Books on Wheels

BOOKS ON WHEELS

Cooperative Learning Through Thematic Units

Janice McArthur
and
Barbara E. McGuire

1998
Libraries Unlimited, Inc.
Englewood, Colorado

LIBRARIES UNLIMITED, INC.
P.O. Box 6633
Englewood, CO 80155-6633
1-800-237-6124
www.lu.com

Production Editor: Stephen Haenel
Editorial Assistant: Felicity Tucker
Copy Editor: Beth Partin
Proofreader: Matthew Stewart
Typesetter: Michael Florman

Library of Congress Cataloging-in-Publication Data

McArthur, Janice.
    Books on wheels : cooperative learning through thematic units / Janice McArthur and Barbara E. McGuire.
    xi, 169p. 22x28 cm.
    Includes bibliographical references and index.
    ISBN 1-56308-535-6
    1. Children's literature--Study and teaching (Primary)
2. Children--Books and reading. 3. Unit method of teaching.
4. Activity programs in education. 5. School libraries--Activity programs. 6. Interdisciplinary approach in education. I. McGuire, Barbara E. II. Title.
LB1527.M33   1998
372.64'044--dc21   98-15994
                                          CIP

CONTENTS

Welcome to *Books on Wheels.* We have designed this book to give librarians and teachers a complete resource for particular themes. The book contains an annotated bibliography, classroom- and kid-tested activities to be done in other areas of the curriculum with children in the library or classroom, and reproducible pages for extension activities.

In using *Books on Wheels,* the librarian or teacher can take the books listed for a particular theme and move the books into the classroom or move the books to a designated area in the library, putting them together where patrons or teachers and children have access to the books for use in thematic instruction. The books can also be put on a cart, to be wheeled to the classroom or left in a prominent area in the library.

To get you off to a rolling start, each chapter begins with ideas for introducing the theme. Along with fun booktalks is an annotated bibliography of books of interest to children on that theme.

The books listed in the bibliography are rated according to three categories: LP—Lower Primary (grades K–1); MP—Middle Primary (grades 1–2); and UP—Upper Primary (grades 2–3). An asterisk (*) at the end of the annotation means the book is a chapter book, suitable for middle and upper primary children who are *proficient* readers.

Also included in this book is a curriculum idea bank and reproducible pages for each chapter. These can be used in follow-up lessons with the children. These activities also have the same rating as the books to provide guidelines for the use of the activity.

The complete package will allow the librarian or teacher to plan and carry out a thematic unit across the curriculum.

Have you ever been camping in the dark woods, gone on a trip, or met a famous person? Children go through life having many adventures. These adventures take place with friends, pets, and family; many adventures take place at school.

The bibliography is a cross section of books with a wide variety of adventurous main characters, from a polar bear to a boa constrictor. Reading these books will help children realize that they may have had similar adventures and that by using their imaginations, they too can have adventures like those of the main characters. Children will also discover a wide world of adventures just by opening a book!

A Rolling Start

1. To introduce the concept of adventure, show the children advertisements cut from magazines. Ask children to look at the pictures and tell what they think is happening in the pictures. Have children use their imaginations to come up with adventures based on the pictures.

2. Have the children brainstorm words that describe the meaning of *adventure* or are synonyms for the word. The words could be put on a chart and referred to throughout the adventure unit.

3. Have children make a poster advertising the main character of their favorite adventure book. Display it as a bulletin board.

Booktalks

Allard, Harry. *Miss Nelson Is Missing.* Boston: Houghton Mifflin, 1977.

What happens in your class when you have sharing time? When your class has a substitute teacher, how do the students act? The kids in Room 207 were misbehaving again. They were doing things they shouldn't do—flying paper airplanes or throwing spitballs at the ceiling. They were the worst-behaved class in the entire school. They were so rude that Miss Nelson said, "Something will have to be done!"

The next day when the students walked into their classroom, there stood a woman in an ugly black dress. "I am your new teacher, Miss Viola Swamp," she said. They were stunned. When they asked where Miss Nelson was, Miss Swamp told them to get busy with their schoolwork.

Days went by and there was no sign of Miss Nelson. The students missed their teacher and her soft voice. They decided to try and find her but failed. One student thought she might have been eaten by sharks. Another thought Miss Nelson might have gone to Mars. What do you think? Will Miss Nelson return? If she does return, will the students behave better? To find out, read *Miss Nelson Is Missing* by Harry Allard. (LP-UP)

Bartone, Elisa. *Peppe the Lamplighter*. New York: Lothrop, Lee & Shepard, 1993.

What do you think it would be like to live without electricity in our homes or streetlights? Peppe lived many years ago, when there wasn't electricity in a poor part of a large city called Little Italy. He had six sisters and his family was very poor. Peppe knew that he needed to find a job, so he began asking different people, like the butcher, if he could work for them. But they all said he was too young. One day Domenico, the man who lit the streetlights, asked Peppe if he would light the lamps for him while he went to Italy to get his wife.

Peppe was excited that he finally had a job to help his family. When Peppe told his family the good news, his father was not happy. He felt that this wasn't a good job for Peppe. But with his sisters' encouragement, Peppe began his job. Each night he went from lamp to lamp, lighting them with a long stick. As he lit each lamp, he would make a wish for one of his sisters' happiness or care.

One day Peppe got discouraged because his father didn't like his job, so he didn't go out to light the lamps. He stayed in the house and wouldn't leave. It grew dark and the streets were not lit. Peppe's young sister Assunta did not come home. The family began to worry, for they knew she wouldn't come home in the dark. Finally Peppe's father begged him to light the lamps. Will Peppe do it? What will happen to Assunta? To find out what Peppe did and what he learned about his job, read *Peppe the Lamplighter* by Elisa Bartone. (LP-UP)

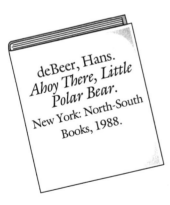

deBeer, Hans. *Ahoy There, Little Polar Bear*. New York: North-South Books, 1988.

Who knows where polar bears live? What do they look like? This is the story of a polar bear named Lars who had a long adventure. Each day he swam and played in the cold Arctic water. But one day as Lars was swimming a long way from his den, or home, he was pulled into a big net with lots of fish. Before Lars knew what was going on, he was on a big ship sailing away from where he lived. Lars climbed out from where the fish were kept to explore the ship. While he was walking around, he met Nemo, the ship's cat. Lars had never seen a ship's cat before, but they soon became friends.

The ship sailed into a harbor, and Lars wondered if he would get back home to see his parents and his home. Nemo introduced Lars to some other cats who lived on ships. They were friendly like Nemo and agree to help him get home. Will the cats be able to help Lars? Will Lars be able to find his home and parents again? To find out what happens to Lars, read *Ahoy There, Little Polar Bear* by Hans deBeer. (LP-MP)

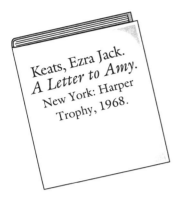

Keats, Ezra Jack. *A Letter to Amy.* New York: Harper Trophy, 1968.

Have you ever received a letter in the mail or written a letter to someone? Peter decides to write a letter to Amy and invite her to his party.

Peter finishes the letter and goes out to mail it. His mother tells him to wear his raincoat because it looks cloudy outside. When Peter gets outside, the storm hits with a flash of lightning and a roll of thunder. Then a gust of wind pulls the envelope out of his hand. That begins an adventure for his letter as the wind whips the envelope through the air. Peter chases it through the streets, trying to catch it. But the letter continues on its adventure as Peter chases it. Then he notices Amy coming toward him. Does he catch it before Amy sees that the letter is for her? What will happen as Peter tries to grab the letter? To find out what happens to Peter and his letter, read *A Letter to Amy* by Ezra Jack Keats. (LP)

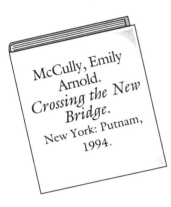

McCully, Emily Arnold. *Crossing the New Bridge.* New York: Putnam, 1994.

Who do you think is happy? Would you be able to find the happiest person in the class? This is what happened long ago to the Mayor of a town by a river. One day the bridge leading into town fell into the river. "We need a new bridge," said the Mayor. The Jubilatti family was brought in to build the bridge. In the middle of deciding how the bridge would be built, an old woman reminded the Mayor of an old tradition, which the Mayor couldn't remember. He was told that the first person to cross the bridge must be the town's happiest person. The Mayor worried. Who was the happiest person? Was it the town banker, the grocer, or someone else? He looked and looked, but soon the bridge was finished and the Mayor still hadn't found the happiest person. What would he do? People couldn't use the bridge until they knew who the happiest person was. How will the mystery be solved? Will the Mayor and town find the happiest person soon so the bridge can be used? To find out if the bridge is saved and if they find the happiest person, read *Crossing the New Bridge* by Emily Arnold McCully. (LP-UP)

Bibliography

Allard, Harry. *Miss Nelson Is Back.* Boston: Houghton Mifflin, 1982.

Miss Nelson told her class that she was going to have her tonsils out and would be gone for a week. The students thought this would be a good time to misbehave, but then they remembered Miss Viola Swamp, the meanest substitute around. They decided they didn't want Miss Swamp for a substitute. (LP-UP)

Allard, Harry. *Miss Nelson Is Missing!* Boston: Houghton Mifflin, 1977.

The students in Miss Nelson's class are rude and disrespectful. What will she do? One day the students come to class and find a new teacher, Miss Viola Swamp. Things change quickly. But where is Miss Nelson? When the students look, they can't find her. (LP-UP)

Allard, Harry. *The Stupids Step Out.* Boston: Houghton Mifflin, 1974.

 The Stupid family decides to go on an outing. As they prepare to go, the family does many silly things to get ready, such as mother wearing the cat as her hat. The Stupid family has a crazy, upside-down, topsy-turvy day. (LP-UP)

Bartone, Elisa. *Peppe the Lamplighter.* New York: Lothrop, Lee & Shepard, 1993.

 Peppe must find a job to help his family, but there are none. Finally he is offered the job of lighting the city street lamps. His father doesn't think this is a good job for Peppe. What will happen if Peppe doesn't light the streetlights to keep the darkness away? (MP-UP)

Brown, Marc. *Arthur Meets the President.* Boston: Joy Street Books, 1991.

 Arthur's class enters a writing contest with the theme, how can you make America great? Arthur's essay wins! This means Arthur, his family, and all his class get to go to Washington, D.C., to meet the president. Arthur is afraid he will forget the speech he has to make to the president. (LP-UP)

Buehner, Caralyn and Mark Buehner. *A Job for Wittilda.* New York: Dial Books for Young Readers, 1993.

 Wittilda is a witch who needs a job. She tries various jobs, but they don't seem to be quite right. She finally gets a job delivering pizza. Will using her broom to deliver the pizza help her keep the job? (LP-UP)

deBeer, Hans. *Ahoy There, Little Polar Bear.* New York: North-South Books, 1988.

 Lars is a baby polar bear who lives on an iceberg in the frozen ocean. One day as he is swimming, he gets caught in a big fishnet and is taken aboard the boat. He meets Nemo, the ship's cat, who helps Lars find his way home. (LP-MP)

Freeman, Don. *Corduroy.* New York: Viking, 1968.

 Corduroy sits on a shelf in a department store, but no one will buy him because he has a button missing. One night when the store is closed, he looks for a button but can't find one.

Then a little girl comes to the store and wants to buy him so he will have a home. (LP-MP)

Keats, Ezra Jack. *A Letter to Amy.* New York: Harper Trophy, 1968.

 Peter wants to invite his friend Amy to his party on Saturday. He writes her a letter. When he goes outside to mail the letter, a rainstorm hits and the letter is whipped out of his hand. As he chases the letter down the street, he sees Amy. He tries to catch the letter before Amy realizes it is for her. (LP)

Keats, Ezra Jack. *Goggles.* New York: Macmillan, 1969.

 Some friends find some broken goggles. These goggles lead the boys into many adventures as they attempt to keep some neighborhood bullies from taking the goggles away from them. (LP-MP)

Leigh, Nila. *Learning to Swim in Swaziland: A Child's Eye View of a Southern African Country.* New York: Scholastic, 1993.

 This is the story of Nila, who moved to Swaziland when she was eight. What does the school she goes to look like? Did you know that water drains in a different direction in this country? Nila talks about her adventures in Swaziland. (MP-UP)

Lionni, Leo. *Inch by Inch.* New York: Mulberry Books, 1995.

 One day a robin is about to eat a worm when the worm says, "Don't eat me. I am an inch worm and I can measure things." The robin, not believing, tells the worm to measure his tail. The worm goes on to measure other animals. (LP-MP).

McCully, Emily Arnold. *Crossing the New Bridge.* New York: Putnam, 1994.

 A long time ago, in a town by a river, the bridge falls into the river and needs to be rebuilt. An old woman tells the Mayor that the happiest person in the village must cross the bridge first. The search begins to find the happiest person in the village, so other villagers can use the bridge. (LP-UP)

Mochizuki, Ken. *Baseball Saved Us.* New York: Lee & Low, 1993.

During World War II, most Japanese Americans were placed in camps away from the West Coast. The Japanese people in the desert camp learned to play baseball to have something to do. This is a story about how learning something well can overcome prejudice. (UP)*

Munsch, Robert. *Thomas' Snowsuit.* Toronto: Annick Press Ltd., 1985.

Thomas's mother buys him a brown snowsuit, which he refuses to wear. After a real struggle with his mother, Thomas ends up with the suit on. When he wears it to school, after a real struggle with his teacher, the snowsuit ends up on his teacher. What will happen when the principal comes in to see what is going on? (LP-UP)

Nichol, Barbara. *Beethoven Lives Upstairs.* New York: Orchard, 1994.

The year is 1822 and Christoph lives in Vienna. He writes to his uncle to tell him that a madman has moved into the rented room upstairs. His uncle writes back that Beethoven is a musician, not a madman. (MP-UP)

Noble, Trinka Hakes. *Jimmy's Boa and the Big Splash Birthday Bash.* New York: Dial Books for Young Readers, 1989.

Maggie came home from Jimmy's birthday party talking about an adventure that happened when they went to Sea Land. The children swam with the seals and the sharks and caused all kinds of problems at Sea Land as Jimmy's boa got into the act. (MP-UP)

Noble, Trinka Hakes. *The Day Jimmy's Boa Ate the Wash.* New York: Dial Press, 1980.

Jimmy's class goes on a field trip to the farm. All kind of things happen: pigs cry and haystacks fall on the cows. Jimmy's boa gets loose and causes even more problems on the farm. (LP-UP).

Polacco, Patricia. *My Rotten Redheaded Older Brother.* New York: Simon & Schuster Books for Young Readers, 1994.

Treesha lives on a farm in Michigan with her older brother, mother, and grandmother. Treesha has many adventures trying to show her brother that she can do something that he can't do. (LP-UP)

Rey, Margaret E. and H. A. Rey. *Curious George Flies a Kite.* Boston: Houghton Mifflin, 1958.

George the curious monkey sees a kite and decides he wants to learn to fly one. George has a big adventure when he flies his kite. (LP-MP)

Steig, William. *Doctor DeSoto.* New York: Farrar, Straus & Giroux, 1982.

Dr. DeSoto is a dentist who treats all animals except those that are enemies of mice. One day a fox comes and pleads with Dr. DeSoto to help him because he has such a terrible toothache. The Doctor agrees and treats the fox, but can he trust him? Dr. DeSoto and his wife try to outfox the fox. (LP-UP)

Steig, William. *Doctor DeSoto Goes to Africa.* New York: HarperCollins, 1992.

Dr. DeSoto, a world-renowned dentist, receives a cablegram asking him to come to Africa to treat an elephant with a toothache. The cablegram says that no one else can care for this elephant. Will Dr. DeSoto be able to help? (LP-UP)

Wood, Audrey. *King Bidgood's in the Bathtub.* San Diego: Harcourt Brace Jovanovich, 1985.

King Bidgood is in the bathtub and won't get out because he is having so much fun. But he is needed to do his kingly duties. All the wise men of the land try to think of ways to get the King out of the bathtub, but nothing seems to work. What can be done to get King Bidgood out of the bathtub? (LP-UP)

Wheeling Across the Curriculum

Critical Thinking

- Give children slips of paper with an adventure, such as "camping in the mountains," written on them. Then they can work in groups to brainstorm what they will need to take on the adventure to make it safe and fun. (MP-UP)

Drama

- Children can act out the events of a story. *The Day Jimmy's Boa Ate the Wash* by Trinka Hakes Noble would work well for this activity. (MP-UP)

Language Arts/Writing

- Many adventure books feature animals as characters. Have children pick an animal and write a story about an adventure the animal may have. (LP-UP)

- Divide children into groups of six. Give them a story starter such as, "On my way home a . . ." Each child writes a line and then passes the story to another child, who writes another line. After everyone has had a turn, the children read the story to the group. (UP)

- On pieces of paper, write opening lines such as "I looked out my window and . . ." Have children draw the slips out of a cup and write an adventure story using the story line. Children in younger grades can tell their stories after choosing pieces of paper with starter lines on them instead of writing them. (LP-UP)

- Have children write a letter telling Miss Nelson how the class's behavior will change if she returns to school. (LP-UP)

- Children can keep a journal of the adventures they have during a specific period, such as a week. These can be shared with the group. (MP-UP)

- Children can decide what questions they would ask a famous person if they had a chance to meet the person. A mock interview can take place after the questions are written. (LP-UP)

- Children can write a letter to friends asking them about adventures they may have had. (LP-UP)

- Read *King Bidgood's in the Bathtub* by Audrey Wood to children and give them a problem they must solve. This can be done individually or in groups. (MP-UP)

- Ask children to pick a piece of clothing and write about an adventure they could have while wearing this article of clothing. (LP-UP)

Mathematics

- The book *Inch by Inch* by Leo Lionni lends itself to doing measuring activities. Have children measure various objects to see how many inches long they are. (LP-UP)

Music

- After they listen to some of Beethoven's music, children can write or draw what adventures the music makes them think about. (LP-UP)

Science

- Children can go outside to look at the clouds and see what shapes they make. They can then write about adventures the shapes (clouds) may have. (LP-UP)

- Children can research various kinds of kites and then make kites of their own. (LP-UP)

Social Studies/Creative Writing

- After doing research on a foreign country, children can work in groups to write a play about an adventure in that country. (UP)

Treasure Maps

Social Studies (UP)

Directions: Pretend you have hidden a treasure. Draw a map showing how to find the treasure. Make sure there are streams and other obstacles on your map so the person following it has an adventure. After reading the map, write about your adventure.

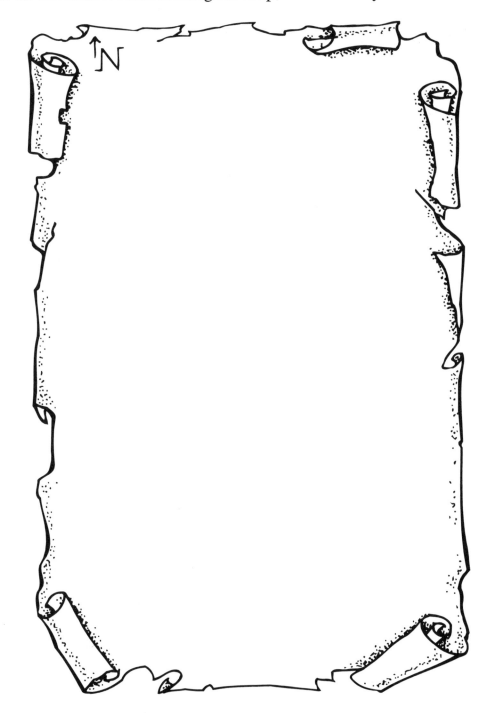

Adventure Story

Art/Language Arts (MP-UP)

Directions: Write and illustrate an adventure story. Draw your illustrations. Then write your story on the line inside the box.

My Adventure

Language Arts (LP-UP)

Directions: Next to each figure write a brief adventure that could take place.

When I spin a web I . . .

On my adventure I saw . . .

When I am in the bathtub . . .

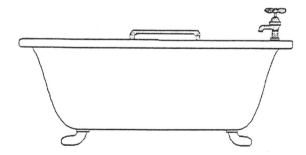

Children love the animals found on a farm or those traditionally associated with it. They laugh at woolly lambs, calves, and other animals. In this chapter, there are books about animals doing traditional farm animal things as well as books about animals doing such things as playing in the snow, being a farmer, or going shopping.

A Rolling Start

1. Have children compare fact and fiction or real and make-believe. Many animals in farm animal stories talk or take on other human characteristics. Children need to understand what animals do in real life and what is make-believe.

2. To introduce children to the books in this genre, a picture of a farm can be put up on a bulletin board. The titles of books can be written on the animals. For example, *Six Creepy Sheep* would be written on a sheep. An adaptation would be to have children write the titles on the farm animals as they read books and add the animals to the bulletin board.

3. Children can make a chart to show the animals that belong on a farm. This will help them classify and focus on which type of animals they are going to be reading about.

Booktalks

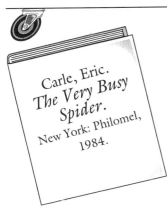

Carle, Eric. *The Very Busy Spider.* New York: Philomel, 1984.

Early in the morning, the spider landed in the farm yard. After landing, she began weaving her silky web. As she wove, the horse, cow, sheep, goat, pig, dog, duck, and rooster all tried to get the spider to go with them on an adventure. The spider just kept right on weaving her web. She wanted to finish before nightfall and catch a fly in her web.

The spider worked all day to finish her web. Will she catch the fly when she finishes? What will happen when the web is done?

As you read the book you can feel the web and watch it grow as the spider is busy spinning it. To learn more about the spider and her web, read *The Very Busy Spider* by Eric Carle. (LP-UP)

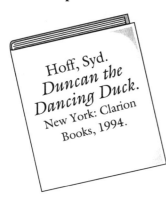

Duncan started dancing in his pond. It was so much fun that he didn't want to stop dancing even when his mother asked. He danced out of the pond and around the farm. The animals kept right on doing what they were doing, ignoring Duncan. He just kept dancing right into the farmhouse. While the farmer and his wife watched, Duncan danced through the house. They felt others should see him dance, so they took Duncan to town. He danced onstage and at a television station. People loved him and followed him wherever he went. Duncan won an award for his dancing. Will Duncan keep dancing? Does he miss the farm? To find out, read *Duncan the Dancing Duck* by Syd Hoff. (LP-MP)

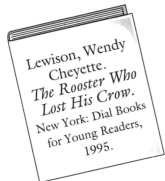

As the sun was just coming up, the Rooster hurried through the farmyard to his place on the fence. He let out his COCK-A-DOODLE-DOO! This was the signal for the farmer to get up and do the morning chores. The farmer would gather the eggs and feed the animals.

One morning Rooster was getting ready to crow, when a bee flew right up to him as he opened his mouth. This scared Rooster, and when he tried to crow nothing came out. He had lost his COCK-A-DOODLE-DOO! He began looking for it all over the farmyard, but he couldn't find it anywhere. He couldn't crow to give the signal for the farmer to get up and begin his chores.

No matter where he looked, the rooster couldn't find his crow. He was upset. Then he heard a lot of noise coming from the chicken house. What was happening? What will Rooster do? Will he get his COCK-A-DOODLE-DOO! back in time to help the chickens? To find out, read *The Rooster Who Lost His Crow* by Wendy Cheyette Lewison. (LP-UP)

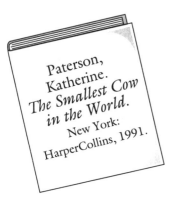

Have you ever heard of a mean cow? On Brock's Dairy Farm, one of the 97 cows was called Rosie. She was so mean she would butt the dog, step on people's feet, and push Mr. Brock into the wall. Marvin was the only person who liked her. He thought she was beautiful. Marvin's sister thought he felt this way because he didn't have to take care of her. But Marvin thought Rosie was so mad because Mr. Brock had sold her calf.

In the spring something happened! Mr. Brock decided to sell Rosie and the farm. He said he wanted to move to a warm, sunny place. Everyone was sad to leave the farm, but Marvin was saddest of all because he missed Rosie.

They settled on their new farm, but Marvin was still very unhappy. Soon strange things began to happen around the farm. There were drawings of cows on walls, the plants in the garden were uprooted, and books were thrown all over. What happened? Everybody started looking for Marvin, thinking he had caused the mischief. But Marvin said it was Rosie who did it. She had become the smallest cow in the world. To find out what happens to Rosie and Marvin, read *The Smallest Cow in the World* by Katherine Paterson. (LP-UP)*

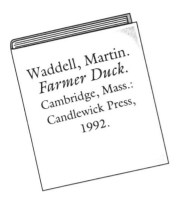

Waddell, Martin. *Farmer Duck.* Cambridge, Mass.: Candlewick Press, 1992.

Have you heard of a duck that is a farmer? In this story, there was a farmer who was very lazy and lay in bed all day. Duck had to do all the work. He brought in the cows from the field and cleaned out the barn. Soon Duck got very upset about having to work so hard all day. The farm animals loved the duck because he worked so hard to take care of them. They held a meeting and decided on a plan to help Duck.

The next morning when Duck went out to begin his chores, he expected the farmer to yell at him as he usually did. No one did. He kept on with the chores, but this time the other farm animals helped him with the work. Was this part of the plan? To find out, read Martin Waddell's book *Farmer Duck.* (LP-UP)

Bibliography

Auch, Mary Jane. *Peeping Beauty.* New York: Holiday House, 1993.

Poulette lived in the farmyard, but she wanted to be a famous ballerina. Each morning, with the other chickens looking on, she did her stretching exercises. One day a fox appeared at the farm and asked Poulette if she had ever been onstage. (LP-UP)

Carle, Eric. *Rooster Who Set Off to See the World.* New York: F. Watts, 1972.

Rooster decides he wants to see the world. He begins his journey. As he travels he meets different animals who want to travel with him. Readers can count the animals who travel with him. (LP-UP)

Carle, Eric. *The Very Busy Spider.* New York: Philomel, 1984.

One day a spider landed in the farmyard and began to spin a web. As she worked, the farm animals came up and asked the spider to join them on an adventure. But the spider kept spinning her web, trying to finish by nightfall. (LP-UP)

Enderle, Judith Ross and Stephanie Gordon Tessler. *Six Creepy Sheep.* New York: Puffin Books, 1993.

One Halloween, six sheep decide to dress and go trick-or-treating. They go out dressed in sheets and pass pirates, fairies, and other scary things. What happens to the sheep as the night progresses? How many sheep will go trick-or-treating? (LP)

Enderle, Judith Ross and Stephanie Gordon Tessler. *Six Snowy Sheep.* New York: Puffin Books, 1995.

On a wintry Christmas day, six sheep decided to play in the snow. One sheep went down the hill on his sled, right into a snowbank. One by one the sheep disappeared into a snowbank. (LP)

Fleischman, Paul. *The Animal Hedge.* New York: E. P. Dutton, 1983.

There was a farmer who loved to watch the baby animals grow up. But one spring there was no rain. It was hard for the animals because there was very little food or water for them. Because he couldn't feed them, the farmer took the animals to market one by one. He missed his animals so much that he decided to make a hedge that looked like his animals. (MP-UP)

Fleischman, Sid. *The Scarebird.* New York: Greenwillow Books, 1988.

There was once a farmer called Lonesome John who lived on a farm all by himself. He made a scarecrow for the corn patch by stuffing straw into his pants, shirt, and other clothes. One day, a young man showed up at the farm. He needed a place to stay and clothes. What will the farmer do to help the young man? (MP-UP)

Fox, Mem. *Hattie and the Fox*. New York: Bradbury Press, 1987.

Hattie was a big black hen. One day she spied a nose in the bushes on the farm. The other animals noticed something, too. Soon the animals saw more than a nose. What are all the animals in the farmyard seeing? (LP-UP)

Griffith, Helen V. *Grandaddy and Janetta*. New York: Greenwillow Books, 1993.

It has been a year since Janetta saw her grandfather and visited his farm. She gets to ride the train all by herself to his farm in Georgia. What happens when she finally reaches Georgia and her grandfather's farm? (MP-UP)*

Griffith, Helen V. *Grandaddy's Place*. New York: Greenwillow Books, 1987.

Janetta and her mother ride the train to visit Janetta's grandfather. She meets her Grandfather for the first time. After a few days, Janetta loves being with her grandfather and the animals because of the fun activities she does with them. (MP-UP)*

Hoff, Syd. *Duncan the Dancing Duck*. New York: Clarion Books, 1994.

One day Duncan began dancing in the pond. He danced all through the barnyard and into the farmhouse. The farmer and his wife thought Duncan was such a good dancer that ev- eryone should have a chance to see him. (LP-UP)

Lewison, Wendy Cheyette. *The Rooster Who Lost His Crow*. New York: Dial Books for Young Readers, 1995.

Each morning Rooster woke up and made it to the fence to crow his COCK-A-DOODLE-DOO! That was the signal for everyone on the farm to wake up. But one morning, a bee flew right in Rooster's face and scared him. He tried to crow, but nothing would come out. (LP-UP)

McPhail, David. *Pigs Aplenty, Pigs Galore!* New York: Dutton Children's Books, 1993.

One night as a man sat reading, he heard a noise coming from the kitchen. When he went to see what was going on, he found pigs everywhere. Pigs aplenty were in the cupboards and on the floor. The pigs kept arriving! Oh, what to do! (LP-UP)

Nodset, Joan L. *Who Took the Farmer's Hat?* New York: Harper & Row, 1963.

The farmer had an old brown hat that he liked very much. One day the wind carried it away. He began to look for his hat, asking all the farm animals if they had seen it. They all told him they hadn't seen the hat. (LP-UP)

Paterson, Katherine. *The Smallest Cow in the World*. New York: HarperCollins, 1991.

Marvin lived on a farm with his family and Rosie, who was the meanest cow in the world. Marvin was sad because the farm was sold and they had to move. On their new farm, strange things began to happen, which Marvin blamed on Rosie. He said Rosie had come back, but no one believed him because they couldn't see Rosie. (MP-UP)*

Peet, Bill. *Chester the Worldly Pig*. Boston: Houghton Mifflin, 1965.

Chester didn't want to be a pig. He felt pigs didn't amount to much. Then he decided to do something about it! After seeing a poster about the circus, he decided to become a circus star. But first he had to learn a trick. (UP)*

Shaw, Nancy. *Sheep in a Shop*. Boston: Houghton Mifflin, 1991.

Five sheep learn that a birthday is coming. They go to a shop to buy some presents. They climb and tumble, making a jumble of the shop. (LP-UP)

Speed, Toby. *Two Cool Cows*. New York: Putnam, 1995.

There were two cool cows from Hucka-buck Farm named Millie and Maude. They wore eight black boots that were cool. What were these two cool cows marching up the hill to do? Were they going to jump over the moon? (LP-UP)

Sundgaard, Arnold. *The Lamb and the Butterfly*. New York: Orchard, 1988.

A lamb met a butterfly and asked about his life. Each time the butterfly flew away, the lamb followed, asking questions. When the butterfly finally left, the lamb was very sad. (LP-UP)

Teague, Mark. *Pigsty*. New York: Scholastic, 1994.

Wendell's mother tells him to clean his room because it is turning into a pigsty. Sure enough, when Wendell goes upstairs, a large pig is lying on his bed! If Wendell doesn't clean his room, will the pigs move in and take over? (LP-UP)

Waddell, Martin. *Farmer Duck*. Cambridge, Mass.: Candlewick Press, 1992.

Can you imagine a farmer who was so lazy that he stayed in bed all day? Duck had to do all the work on the farm. The other farm animals felt sorry for Duck because he worked so hard, and they developed a plan to help the Duck. (LP-UP)

Weidt, Maryann. *Daddy Played Music for the Cows*. New York: Lothrop, Lee & Shepard, 1995.

This is the story of a girl who lives on a farm. Her father always played music in the barn for the cows. As a baby she sat in a play-pen, listening to the cows and the music while her father milked the cows. As she grew older, she helped with the cows and played in the barn, listening and singing to the music. (LP-UP)

Wheeling Across the Curriculum

Art

- Children can make a sheep using cotton balls for the fur. (LP)

- Children can make a diorama of a farm. Plastic animals can be used, or they can be made out of clay. (MP-UP)

- A mural showing farm animals and a farm can be made by the children. (LP-UP)

- Children can make a flip book with farm animal pictures. Each page can be cut in thirds so that "unique" animals can be made by flipping the pictures to mix up the heads, bodies, and feet. (MP-UP)

- Children can make a stuffed farm animal by drawing the front and back of the animal on cloth or butcher paper, cutting it out, sewing it together, and then stuffing it with old newspaper. (LP-UP)

- After reading *The Very Busy Spider* by Eric Carle, children can make their own spider web by applying white glue to black construction paper. When it dries the web is visible. (LP-UP)

Critical Thinking

- Charts or lists can be generated by children to show the different characteristics of the farm animals. (LP-UP)

- Before beginning a unit on farm animals, children can brainstorm on what they already know about farm animals. (LP-UP)

Language Arts/Writing

- Children can write a journal entry about a day in the life of a specific farm animal. (LP-UP)

- Write the names of the different farm animals on pieces of paper. Children can pick a piece of paper and then write a story about the animal. (LP-UP)

- Children can do research on a particular farm animal. Then they can write a report on their findings or display what they have learned on a bulletin board. (UP)

Listening

- Record the sounds of farm animals. As they are played, have the children hold up a picture of the farm animal that makes the sound. (LP)

Mathematics

- Children can make charts and graphs showing which farm animal eats the most for its size. (UP)

- After reading *Six Creepy Sheep* and *Six Snowy Sheep* by Judith Ross Enderle and Stephanie Gordon Tessler, children can do math activities. (LP-MP)

- Children can make up math problems using cows and boots after reading *Two Cool Cows* by Toby Speed. (LP-UP)

- Math problems related to farm animals can be developed for children. For example, ask the children, if a chicken produces two eggs a day, how many will it produce in a month? (MP-UP)

Music

- Young children can learn the song "Old MacDonald Had a Farm." As they sing about each animal, the children can hold up a picture of the animal. (LP)

Science/Social Studies

- Children can do research to find out what different products, such as milk and meat from cows, come from farm animals. (MP-UP)

Create-a-Puppet

Art/Language Arts (LP-UP)

Directions: Add ears, nose, and mouth to create your own farm animal puppet. Attach it to a wooden stick. Write a story about your animal.

Farm Math

Mathematics (MP-UP)

1. The cows eat feed in 10-pound bags. If a cow eats one bag each day, how many bags will 30 cows eat in a day?_____
    How many pounds of food do all the cows eat?

    _____

2. There are 50 chickens on the farm, each laying one egg a day. How many eggs are laid each day?_____ How many eggs will be laid in a week?_____

3. If the eggs laid by the chickens in problem 2 sell for 5 cents each, how much will the farmer receive each day?_____How much will he receive for a week's worth of eggs?

    _____

4. Make up your own problem using farm animals. Share your problem with a friend.

Farm Animal Venn Diagram

Critical Thinking (MP-UP)

Directions: List the characteristics of four-legged farm animals in the left circle. List those of the two-legged animals on the right. Write those characteristics that are the same in the middle area.

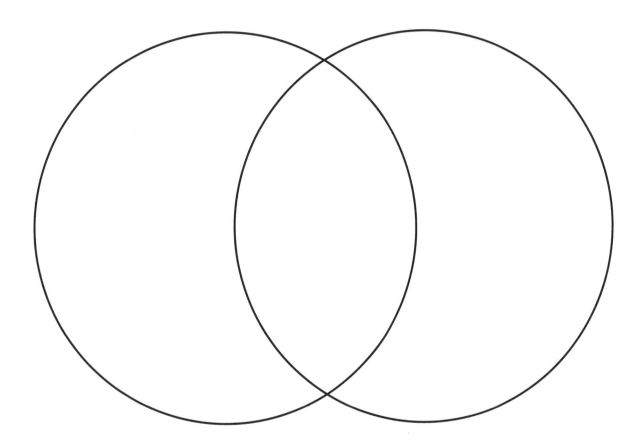

Four-legged farm animals   Two-legged farm animals

The Caldecott Award is given annually to the artist whose illustrations are judged best by the Children's Services of the American Library Association. Started in 1938, the award is named for Randolph Caldecott, a nineteenth-century author. His illustrations showed that children's books could be fun and that illustrations could help tell the story.

The books in this chapter have been chosen as a representative sample of Caldecott Award–winning books. They span the 60 years since the award was first given. Many of the curriculum ideas are based on illustrating.

A Rolling Start

1. Introduce children to Randolph Caldecott. Show a picture of him and his illustrations, so children can understand why the award was named after him.

2. Teach children how illustrations can tell or enhance a story. Show the children a wordless picture book or a book with very few words, such as *Tuesday* by David Wiesner. After reading the book to the children, have them discuss how the illustrations helped them know what was happening in the story.

3. Using book jackets, make a bulletin board of Caldecott Award–winning books. The bulletin board could also contain drawings by children of their favorite part of a Caldecott book. Children could also make their own book jackets to put up on the bulletin board.

Booktalks

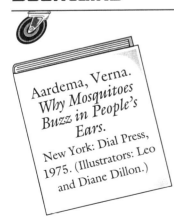

Aardema, Verna. *Why Mosquitoes Buzz in People's Ears.* New York: Dial Press, 1975. (Illustrators: Leo and Diane Dillon.)

Have you ever had a mosquito bother you? How did you know it was a mosquito? This is a story from West Africa that tells of the mischief the mosquito caused for all the animals.

One day the Iguana was going through the forest, and the Mosquito began telling him a big story. The Iguana got mad and didn't want to listen, so he put sticks in his ears. The Python saw the Iguana as he was slithering through the jungle. Iguana didn't answer him when he said "good morning," so Python knew something was dreadfully wrong. He spied a hole in the ground and wiggled into it, scaring the Rabbit who lived there. This set off a series of events that caused problems for the animals of the jungle.

The Lion, King of all the animals, tried to find out what caused such problems. As each animal related what happened, the Lion realized there was no easy answer. The animals decided that it was the Mosquito's fault. He was the cause of all the chaos and problems.

To find out why mosquitoes bother people with their pesky buzz, read *Why Mosquitoes Buzz in People's Ears* by Verna Aardema.

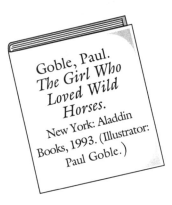

Goble, Paul. *The Girl Who Loved Wild Horses.* New York: Aladdin Books, 1993. (Illustrator: Paul Goble.)

Native Americans have long loved horses. In the old days, they followed the wild horses as they roamed in herds. This is the story of a girl from a Native American tribe that had horses. The girl loved the tribe's horses and took care of them. One day, while the girl was with the horses, there was a terrible thunderstorm. The storm frightened the horses, and they started to run. The girl grabbed the mane of one of the horses and jumped on its back. She rode off with the horses, who joined a herd of wild horses living nearby. The girl lived with the wild horses for many months. She was seen riding one of the wild horses and leading a colt. How long will she be with the horses? Will the members of her family and the tribe be able to find her and bring her home? Read the story *The Girl Who Loved Wild Horses* by Paul Goble to find out what happens to the girl in this story about Native Americans.

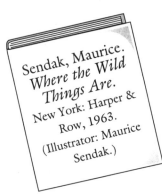

Sendak, Maurice. *Where the Wild Things Are.* New York: Harper & Row, 1963. (Illustrator: Maurice Sendak.)

What kind of adventures do you have? Have you ever gone to bed without supper and had a wild rumpus? That is what happened to Max. He put on his wolf suit one night and was sent to bed for roaring at his mother. Then he sailed off through night and day, until he came to the place where the wild things lived. There his adventure began. The wild things made him King, and the wild rumpus began. They danced and sang, roared their terrible roars, and gnashed their terrible teeth. The wild rumpus continued, but Max was sad. He missed home. What do you think he did? Did he stay with the wild things or sail back through night and day? Read about Max's adventure in *Where the Wild Things Are* by Maurice Sendak.

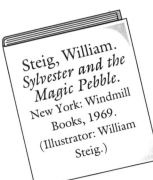

Steig, William. *Sylvester and the Magic Pebble.* New York: Windmill Books, 1969. (Illustrator: William Steig.)

Have you ever seen magic? Have you wished that magic could happen and all your wishes could come true? Sylvester is a little donkey who lives with his parents. He has a happy life, as do most youngsters his age. His hobby is collecting pretty, unusual, or different pebbles.

One day when Sylvester is on vacation, he finds a wonderful pebble that is red and shiny. He soon realizes that when he holds the pebble, anything he wishes for will happen. Sylvester is excited because he thinks his pebble will help his family and friends.

When Sylvester is out walking near his home, he runs into a lion. Naturally, seeing a lion scares Sylvester. Not realizing what he is doing, Sylvester wishes he were a rock so the lion can't get him. The magic pebble is in Sylvester's hand. Can you guess what happens? Right, he turns into a rock. What do you think happens next? Will Sylvester spend the rest of his life as a rock? What do you think his parents did when Sylvester didn't come home? To find out what happens to Sylvester, read the story *Sylvester and the Magic Pebble* by William Steig.

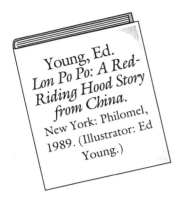

Young, Ed. *Lon Po Po: A Red-Riding Hood Story from China.* New York: Philomel, 1989. (Illustrator: Ed Young.)

Do you have a special name for your grandmother? Do you call her Nana or Granny? In China, the word for grandmother is PoPo. This is the story of three young girls whose mother left them to go visit their grandmother for her birthday. Their mother told the girls to stay in the house and lock the door while she was gone.

There was an old wolf who lived nearby. He saw the mother leave. He knocked on the door. Shang, the oldest, asked, "Who's there?" "Your PoPo," answered the wolf. The two youngest girls were so excited to see their grandmother they almost opened the door. Shang, being more wise, asked whoever was out there, "Our mother has gone to visit you. Did you not see her?" Trying to be sly, the wolf said, "I have not met her along the way. She must have taken a different route." Finally, the little girls opened the door, and the wolf got inside. He quickly blew out the candles so the girls couldn't see him and discover that it really wasn't their PoPo. Now, Shang was not only the oldest, she was also very clever. Before long, she realized the wolf had disguised himself as their beloved PoPo. Will she be able to think of a way to save the three of them from the bad wolf? What will she do? To find out if Shang is wise and clever enough to save herself and her sisters, read *Lon Po Po* by Ed Young.

Bibliography

Aardema, Verna. *Why Mosquitoes Buzz in People's Ears.* New York: Dial Press, 1975. (Illustrators: Leo and Diane Dillon.)

The Mosquito starts trouble in the jungle by trying to tell a big story to the Iguana. When the Iguana doesn't want to listen to the Mosquito's tale, the trouble begins. The Lion tries to get to the reason for the trouble and finds that it is all the Mosquito's fault. (LP-UP)

Bemelmans, Ludwig. *Madeline's Rescue.* New York: Viking, 1953. (Illustrator: Ludwig Bemelmans.)

Madeline lives in Paris at a school with other girls. One day as the girls are out for a walk, Madeline falls into the pond. She is rescued from the pond. Then she is promptly taken back to the school and put to bed. (MP-UP)

Burton, Virginia Lee. *The Little House.* New York: Houghton Mifflin, 1942. (Illustrator: Virginia Lee Burton.)

There was a little house out in the country that was built to last forever. As the years passed, the little house saw many changes as the city grew up around it. The little house wasn't sure all the changes were good and longed to be in the beautiful countryside once again. (LP-MP)

Cendrars, Blaise. *Shadow.* New York: Charles Scribner's Sons, 1982. (Illustrator and translator: Marcia Brown.)

Translated from the French, this book is the story of shadows. These African stories have been told around the village fires there for many years. The shadows change and are found in many different ways and many different places. Through poetry and vivid illustrations, the shadows emerge and can be seen. (UP)

Goble, Paul. *The Girl Who Loved Wild Horses.* New York: Aladdin Books, 1993. (Illustrator: Paul Goble.)

In this Native American story, a girl loves horses and takes care of the horses for a tribe. One day during a thunderstorm, she jumps on a horse's back as the herd flees and rides off with the horses. The girls lives for a very long time with the tribe's horses and the wild horses they meet. (MP-UP)

Hader, Berta and Elmer Hader. *The Big Snow*. New York: Macmillan, 1948. (Illustrators: Berta and Elmer Hader.)

The wild geese head south. The animals of the forest hear them honking as they fly through the sky. They know this means cold weather will soon be coming. Each animal must get ready for winter in its own way. The rabbit must grow a thick coat. The chipmunk stores seeds to get ready for the big snow. (LP-MP)

Hogrogian, Nonny. *One Fine Day*. New York: Macmillan, 1971. (Illustrator: Nonny Hogrogian.)

One fine day the fox was out for a walk. He was very thirsty and saw a pail of milk. An old woman was gathering firewood and didn't see the fox until he drank most of the milk. She was so angry at the fox that she chopped off his tail. The old woman told him that he could get his tail back if he did something for her. (LP-UP)

Keats, Ezra Jack. *The Snowy Day*. New York: Viking, 1962. (Illustrator: Ezra Jack Keats.)

Peter wakes up in the morning to a big snow that fell in the night. While playing in the snow, he sees tracks from many animals, makes snow angels, and has other adventures. Peter learns that many things can be done in the snow. (LP-MP)

Macaulay, David. *Black and White*. Boston: Houghton Mifflin, 1990. (Illustrator: David Macaulay.)

Have you ever tried to read four stories at once? This book contains four stories and illustrations to go along with each one. Are the stories about four separate subjects? Or are they interrelated in some way? Read this story and look at the illustrations carefully to figure out the story. (UP)

McCloskey, Robert. *Make Way for Ducklings*. New York: Viking, 1941. (Illustrator: Robert McCloskey.)

Mother duck wants to take her ducklings to the pond in the park to teach them how to swim. But she must take them across a very busy street to get to the park. How will the ducklings get there? Can they get to the pond safely? (LP-MP)

McCloskey, Robert. *Time of Wonder*. New York: Viking, 1957. (Illustrator: Robert McCloskey.)

The weather causes all kinds of wonderful things to happen. This story takes place in Maine. You can stand on the shore and see the rain getting closer, or you can watch the waves. Sometimes it is foggy and the sun tries to peek through. Then the seasons change. (LP-UP)

McDermott, Gerald. *Arrow to the Sun*. New York: Viking, 1974. (Adaptor and illustrator: Gerald McDermott.)

This story is a Native American creation story. It is based on the Pueblo tribe's belief about how people came to be. The beautiful illustrations enhance the story. They tell of the beginning of man showing the sun as the center of the story of human creation. (MP-UP)

Mosel, Arlene, retold by *The Funny Little Woman*. New York: Dutton Children's Books, 1972. (Illustrator: Blair Lent.)

This is a story from ancient Japan about a little woman who used to make dumplings and tea. One day a dumpling rolls through a hole. She finds herself on a strange road under the earth, where there are lots of unusual characters. (MP-UP)

Musgrove, Margaret. *Ashanti to Zulu: African Traditions*. New York: Dial Press, 1976. (Illustrators: Leo and Diane Dillon.)

This book takes each letter of the alphabet and introduces it by telling an African tradition that begins with that letter. The illustrations also teach much about African art. (UP)

Ness, Evaline. *Sam, Bang and Moonshine*. New York: Holt, Rinehart & Winston, 1966. (Illustrator: Evaline Ness.)

Samantha, or Sam, as she was known, told stories. "Sam said this. Sam said that. Whatever Sam said, you could never believe." Sam told people she had a lion. Really, she had a cat named Bang. But what is this moonshine that Sam is talking about? (LP-UP)

Provensen, Alice and Martin Provensen. *The Glorious Flight: Across the Channel with Louis Bleriot, July 25, 1909.* New York: Viking, 1983. (Illustrators: Alice and Martin Provensen.)

    The year is 1901. Louis Bleriot and his family are out for a drive one day when he sees a flying machine. He knows this is something he must do. In 1909 he flies across the English Channel. (MP-UP)

Sendak, Maurice. *Where the Wild Things Are.* New York: Harper & Row, 1963. (Illustrator: Maurice Sendak.)

    Max is sent to bed while wearing his wolf suit. Soon he has an adventure. He sails across the night and day to where the wild things live. There he is made King of the Wild Things. They have a wild rumpus, and they roar their terrible roars. (LP-MP)

Steig, William. *Sylvester and the Magic Pebble.* New York: Windmill Books, 1969. (Illustrator: William Steig.)

    Sylvester is a little donkey who likes to collect unusual pebbles. One day he finds a red pebble and discovers that it is magical. When Sylvester sees a lion, he is scared. He wishes he were a stone so the lion can't hurt him. He turns into the stone. Will Sylvester have to live forever as a stone? (LP-UP)

Udry, Janice May. *A Tree Is Nice.* New York: Harper, 1956. (Illustrator: Marc Simont.)

    What is a tree good for? This story talks about all the ways a tree can be used. It can give shade. It is good for swinging. How would you use a tree? (LP-MP)

Van Allsburg, Chris. *Jumanji.* Boston: Houghton Mifflin, 1981. (Illustrator: Chris Van Allsburg.)

    Judy and Peter are bored. They decide to go outside. By the foot of a tree, they find a box that says, "Jumanji—A Jungle Adventure." They decide to take the game home and play it. As they begin to play it, strange things take place. (LP-UP)

Van Allsburg, Chris. *Polar Express.* Boston: Houghton Mifflin, 1985. (Illustrator: Chris Van Allsburg.)

    It's Christmas Eve. A boy lies wondering about Santa because his friend told him there was no Santa. He hears a steam engine and looks outside to see a train in his front yard. The conductor yells, "All aboard!" The train is going to the North Pole. He wants to find out about Santa, so he gets on board. (LP-UP)

Ward, Lynd. *The Biggest Bear.* Boston: Houghton Mifflin, 1952. (Illustrator: Lynd Ward.)

    Johnny Orchard lives on a farm. He feels humiliated because all the other farms in the area have a bearskin tacked to the barn wall. Johnny decides to find the biggest bear he can and shoot it. Then he can put the skin on the barn. But instead of finding the biggest bear, he finds a cub. (LP-MP)

Wiesner, David. *Tuesday.* New York: Clarion, 1991. (Illustrator: David Wiesner.)

    In this book, the frogs live on their lily pads during the day. But at night, they leave their lily pads and go exploring. While their neighbors are sound asleep, the frogs visit. The intricate illustrations are what tell the story in this book. (MP-UP)

Yolen, Jane. *Owl Moon.* New York: Philomel, 1987. (Illustrator: John Schoenherr.)

    Looking for owls late at night is called "owling." One night, a little girl and her father go owling. They hear lots of sounds in the night as they trudge through the snow looking for owls. They try to be quiet so they can find owls. Because of the bright, yellow moon, they see lots of things on this winter night. (LP-UP)

Yorinks, Arthur. *Hey Al.* New York: Farrar, Straus & Giroux, 1986. (Illustrator: Richard Egielski.)

Al is a janitor who lives with his dog Eddie. They live in a tiny, one-room apartment. Life is a struggle. They are unhappy until a mysterious bird transports them to a special island in the sky. Everything is wonderful for a while, but life on the island changes. Al realizes his old life wasn't quite so bad. Will he get back to his apartment and job? (LP-UP)

Young, Ed. *Lon Po Po: A Red-Riding Hood Story from China.* New York: Philomel, 1989. (Illustrator: Ed Young.)

Mother leaves her three daughters while she goes to visit Grandmother (or PoPo, as she is called in Chinese). But a sly wolf is watching and decides that the three girls will make a good meal. Shang is the oldest and wisest daughter. Will she figure out a way to save herself and her sisters from the wolf? (LP-UP)

Wheeling Across the Curriculum

Art

- Children can make their own wordless picture book by drawing pictures to tell a story. (LP-UP)

- Study one illustrator, such as Maurice Sendak, to determine how the illustrations are done. (MP-UP)

- Compare illustrations from several different illustrators for style, color, or materials used. (UP)

- Look at art media such as collage, watercolors, or pen and ink so children can learn the different ways illustrations can be done. (MP-UP)

- Have children design their own Wild Thing. Make it two-sided and have them stuff it with newspaper. (LP-MP)

- Children can make paper bag puppets of the animals in *Why Mosquitoes Buzz in People's Ears* by Verna Aardema and then act out the story. (LP-UP)

- Children can use cotton balls to make a snow scene. (LP-UP)

- Have an illustrating contest. Ask children to illustrate a short story. Have judges from outside the classroom determine the "Caldecott Winner" for the class. (MP-UP)

- Children can choose a pebble and paint it to make their own magic pebble. They can write about the magic spells it has. (LP-UP)

- Children can study art from China after reading *Lon Po Po.* (UP)

- Native American art can be studied after reading *The Girl Who Loved Wild Horses* by Paul Goble and *Arrow to the Sun* by Gerald McDermott. (MP-UP)

Language Arts/Writing

- Children can write about what they would wish for if they had a magic pebble. (MP-UP)

- Children can write a story and make a collage to illustrate it. (UP)

- Using a sequence of pictures with no text, have children write a story based on the pictures. (LP-UP)

- The traditions of other countries can be studied. Children can also write about their family traditions.(LP)

- Several of the Caldecott books have stories that use repetition to build upon and emphasize a theme. Read one of these stories with a problem that builds and then is solved. Then have children write a story of their own with the same structure. (UP)

- Have children make a drawing of tree. Then they can write a story about all the things that happen to the tree or all the things the tree has seen in its life. (MP-UP)

Mathematics

- Have children make a collage of variously sized geometric shapes cut from construction paper. (LP-UP)

Music

- After reading *Ashanti to Zulu* by Margaret Musgrove, children can listen to African music and learn African songs. (LP-UP)

Science

- Children can study the different types of tracks made by animals in the snow or sand after reading *The Snowy Day* by Ezra Jack Keats. (MP-UP)

- After reading *The Big Snow* by Berta and Elmer Hader, children can do research to determine what animals must do to get ready for winter and what changes may take place in their bodies. (UP)

- *Time of Wonder* by Robert McCloskey lends itself to having children study about the weather and changes in the seasons. (LP-UP)

Social Studies

- Children can work in cooperative learning groups to develop a game after reading *Jumanji* by Chris Van Allsburg. (UP)

- Map skills can be studied after children read the books about other countries, such as *Lon Po Po* by Ed Young or *Madeline's Rescue* by Ludwig Bemelmans. (UP)

- Research can be done to find out more about the various Native American tribes in the United States and where they live. (UP)

- The cultures discussed in several of the books in this chapter have different forms of traditional dress. After children research these, then they can make paper doll clothes representative of the cultures. (MP-UP)

Geo Shapes

Mathematics/Art (LP-UP)

What kind of pictures can be made from these geometric shapes?
Directions: Cut out the geometric shapes and use as many as you can to make illustrations for a story.

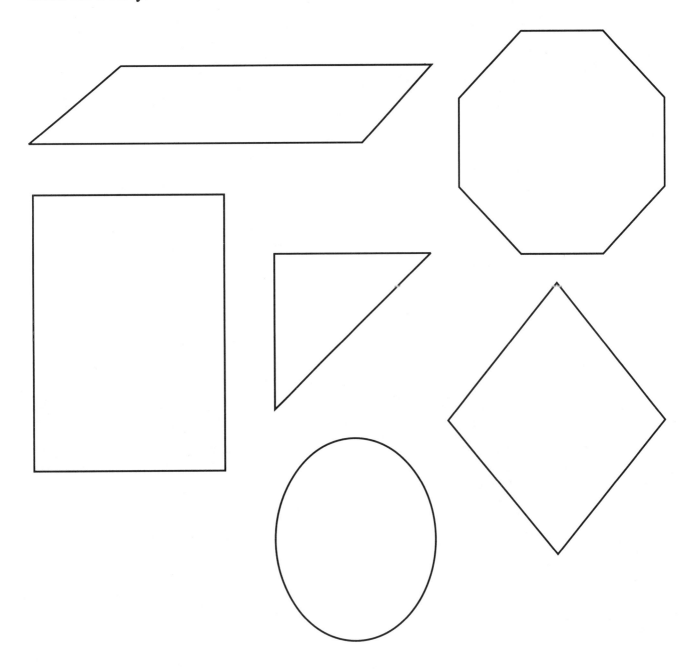

Award Winners I Have Read

Reading (LP-UP)

Directions: Write the titles of the Caldecott Award–winning books you have read by the word "Title." On the next line, write the name of the illustrator. On the following lines, write what you liked—or disliked—about the book.

Title: _____

Illustrator: _____

_____

_____

_____

_____

_____

Wishing Pebbles

Language Arts (LP-UP)

Remember what happened to Sylvester when he wished on his magic pebble?
Directions: On each pebble, write what you would wish for if you had three wishes.

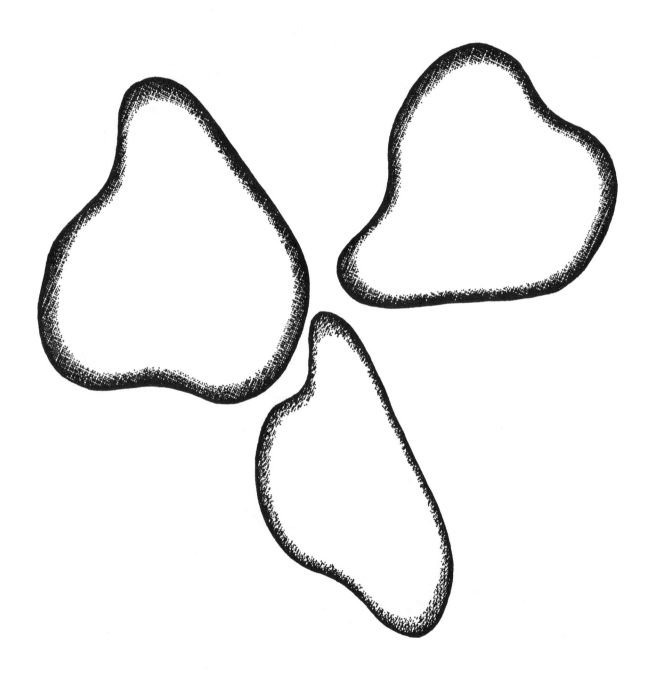

..⚑OUT OF THE PAST: DINOSAURS

CHAPTER 4

Out of the past! What a fascination children have with dinosaurs. They seem to be a perennial favorite. This chapter looks at all different types of dinosaur books. The bibliography includes dinosaur alphabet books as well as books that describe the process of digging up dinosaur bones. For those readers who like fiction, there are also books with dinosaurs as the main characters, having many adventures.

A Rolling Start

1. To introduce dinosaurs, have children make a chart to demonstrate what they know about dinosaurs and what they would like to learn. It can be added to as the unit progresses, so children can show their new understanding.

2. Have children draw pictures of what they think dinosaurs look like. They can put them on a bulletin board. The pictures could be re-done or added to after children have learned more about dinosaurs.

3. As children read dinosaur books, they can write the titles on a paper bone. The bones can be hung around the room or pasted on the wall to make the shape of a large dinosaur.

Booktalks

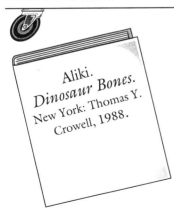

Aliki. *Dinosaur Bones.* New York: Thomas Y. Crowell, 1988.

In 1676, the first dinosaur fossil was mentioned by scientists. This book takes the reader through the history of scientists finding dinosaurs bones and fossils. Scientists worked to put the bones together that were found because they had never seen anything like them before. One of the first scientists who put these bones together was Dr. Gideon Mantell. Another scientist, Dr. Richard Owen, was the person who named these reptiles "Dinosauria," or "terrible lizards," but they were called dinosaurs.

31

The three prehistoric periods in which dinosaurs lived are discussed in the book. The reader learns about the dinosaurs that lived during these periods. To learn more about dinosaurs and the scientists who discovered them, read *Dinosaur Bones* by Aliki. (MP-UP)

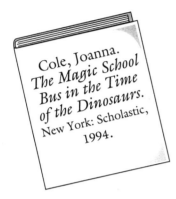

It was visitors' day at the school, and Ms. Frizzle's class was turning their classroom into Dinosaur Land. They had been studying dinosaurs. Ms. Frizzle told the children to get in the school bus. After driving for a long time, they came to a dinosaur dig. At the dig, paleontologists, those scientists who study prehistoric life, were digging to find fossils and dinosaur bones.

Suddenly, Ms. Frizzle and the children entered the time machine and found themselves back in the time when the dinosaurs roamed the earth! What will they see? What kind of dinosaurs will they run into? To find out about dinosaurs and the adventures of Ms. Frizzle's class, read *The Magic School Bus in the Time of the Dinosaurs* by Joanna Cole. (LP-UP)

Long, long ago there were dinosaurs on the earth. Scientists have discovered many facts about dinosaurs. They learned that some dinosaurs were plant eaters and some were meat eaters.

But what was life like before the dinosaurs roamed the earth? In this book, the reader learns that, millions of years before the dinosaurs, there were creatures in the seas like sponges, corals, and snails. There were also the first fish. Their mouths were nothing but small holes, and they had to suck their food because their mouths didn't open or close.

Millions of years went by before plants began to grow on the earth, but still no dinosaurs appeared. This was known as the age of the fishes.

Many different amphibians lived during this period. Plants, trees, and ferns grew in abundance, and animal life could be sustained. These new animals were called reptiles. They evolved into many different types. They became bigger and stronger because they didn't have to live close to the water and there were many different food sources available to reptiles.

In a process called evolution, some of the animals continued to change the way they lived and became the forerunners of the mammals known today.

Still many millions of years passed with no dinosaurs. To find out how and when dinosaurs finally came to live on the earth, read *Before the Dinosaurs* by Miriam Schlein. This book also includes a time chart showing when different forms of animal life appeared on earth. (MP-U)

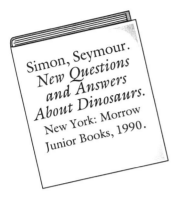

This book is a factual book that answers many questions about dinosaurs. Some of the questions the book answers are: What are dinosaurs? Who first named the dinosaur? How smart were the dinosaurs? What are some new discoveries about dinosaurs?

Along with the factual information, colorful illustrations depict the various types of dinosaurs. This gives the reader an image of what dinosaurs might have looked like.

Do you know that the Saltopus was a dinosaur weighing about 2 pounds and was the size of a cat? There were many small dinosaurs, as well as the very large ones that we are more familiar with.

There have been more than 50 new kinds of dinosaurs discovered over the last few years. Scientists are still finding out new information about dinosaurs.

To find out the answers to all your dinosaur questions, read *New Questions and Answers About Dinosaurs* by Seymour Simon. (LP-UP)

Do you know what a fossil is? Where do you find them? Lucy and Max went on a fossil hunt with their grandfather, the Professor. They found a big bone that gave off a strange light. They decided to camp for the night in a cave because it was late. Suddenly there was a ghostly silver shape. Max thought they were monsters, but the Professor said they were dinosaur ghosts.

As they watched, the ghosts floated by groaning horribly and giving off light. They began running to get away from the dinosaur ghosts. But they were trapped! Will more strange things happen? Will they see more dinosaur ghosts? To find out what happens to Lucy, Max, and the Professor, read *A Night in the Dinosaur Graveyard* by A. J. Wood. This book includes a special surprise for the reader. (LP-UP)

Bibliography

Aliki. *Digging Up Dinosaurs*, New York: Harper Trophy, 1988.

There are lots of dinosaurs bones in museums. This is the story of how dinosaur bones are found, dug up, and then cleaned and put together in the form of a skeleton. This book is designed to give the reader facts about dinosaurs and how they are found. (MP-UP)

Aliki. *Dinosaur Bones*. New York: Thomas Y. Crowell, 1988.

This book tells the story of how dinosaur bones were discovered. The reader learns about how scientists over the years have studied and collected bones. (MP-UP)

Branley, Franklyn M. *What Happened to the Dinosaurs?* New York: Thomas Y. Crowell, 1989.

In easy-to-read text, the author discusses the many theories that scientists have researched to answer the age-old question, "What happened to the dinosaurs?" (LP-MP)

Cohen, Daniel. *Allosaurus and Other Jurassic Meat-Eaters*. Minneapolis: Capstone Press, 1996.

What kinds of dinosaurs lived during the Jurassic period? One was the Allosaurus, a meat eater. Also contained in the book are addresses of where dinosaur tracks can be seen, organizations to write for dinosaur information, and a glossary of terms. (MP-LP)

Cole, Joanna. *The Magic School Bus in the Time of the Dinosaurs*. New York: Scholastic, 1994.

Ms. Frizzle's class was busy making their classroom into Dinosaur Land. Visitors were coming, and the children were setting up displays to show everything they had learned about dinosaurs. (LP-UP)

Dixon, Dougal. *Digging Up the Past: The Search for Dinosaurs*. New York: Thomson Learning, 1995.

This book is divided into sections about the different dinosaurs that roamed the earth. Included in this book is a glossary of terms as well as a time line showing when the dinosaurs lived. (LP-UP)*

Dodson, Peter. *An Alphabet of Dinosaurs*. New York: Scholastic, 1995.

This book has drawings and illustrations of dinosaurs for each letter of the alphabet. The drawings also highlight those parts of each dinosaur that distinguish it from other dinosaurs. The colorful illustrations show the dinosaur in what is believed to be its habitat. (MP-UP)

Donnally, Liza. *Dinosaur's Thanksgiving*. New York: Scholastic, 1995.

Rex and his dog Bones are getting ready for Thanksgiving. After buying a pumpkin pie, they meet a hysilophodon who invites them to a Dinosaur Thanksgiving. Included is a glossary of dinosaurs. This is one of a series of books about dinosaurs and the seasons. (LP-MP)

Funston, Sylvia. *The Dinosaur Question and Answer Book*. Boston: Joy Street Books 1992.

This books is based on a project done by Canadian scientists in Asia and North America. Written in a question-and-answer format, it is a good reference book for children. (LP-UP)

Howard, John. *I Can Read About Dinosaurs*. New York: Troll Associates, 1986.

This book about dinosaurs is designed for young readers in an easy-to-read style. The book also describes how scientists search for fossils today so people can continue to learn about dinosaurs. (LP-MP)

Krueger, Richard. *The Dinosaurs*. Brookfield, Conn.: Millbrook Press, 1995.

This book is written for the more mature reader. The author traces the history of the dinosaur through the three periods to the end of the dinosaur age. (UP)*

Lasky, Kathryn. *Dinosaur Dig*. New York: Morrow Junior Books, 1990.

The illustrations are photographs from a dinosaur dig that took place in Montana. A family that lives in the East dreams of visiting the dig and learning about dinosaurs. This story tells of their adventures on the dig. (LP-UP)

Martin, Linda. *When Dinosaurs Go Visiting*. San Francisco: Chronicle Books, 1993.

What do you do before you go visiting? The dinosaurs wear their nicest clothes and wash carefully so they are clean. They also bring a little gift and cook their favorite dish. (LP-MP)

Most, Bernard. *If the Dinosaurs Came Back*. San Diego: Harcourt Brace Jovanovich, 1978.

This is the fictional story of a boy who loves dinosaurs. He reads and thinks about them, but most of all he wishes the dinosaurs would return to the earth. He thinks of all the ways dinosaurs could be used. The book also contains drawings of the common dinosaurs. (LP-MP)

Most, Bernard. *Whatever Happened to the Dinosaurs?* New York: Harcourt Brace Jovanovich, 1984.

Where did the dinosaurs go? Are they on another planet somewhere? Was there a shortage of food for the dinosaurs? What do you think happened to the dinosaurs? This books talks about some of the possibilities. (LP)

Mullins, Patricia. *Dinosaur Encore.* New York: HarperCollins, 1993.

A picture book about dinosaurs that is created for the young reader. It is illustrated with pages that fold out and open up to give added enjoyment to the reader. (LP)

Pallotta, Jerry. *The Dinosaur Alphabet Book.* Chicago: Children's Press, 1991.

In this book, the letters of the alphabet stand for dinosaurs, from ankylosaurus for A to zephyrosaurus for Z. There is much to learn about dinosaurs as you go through the alphabet. (MP-UP)

Parker, Steve. *Inside Dinosaurs and Other Prehistoric Creatures.* New York: Doubleday Books for Young Readers, 1993.

This book is designed to give the more mature reader many insights into dinosaurs. It discusses the dinosaurs' digestion and brains and what can be learned from their bones. (UP)*

Rohmann, Eric. *Time Flies.* New York: Crown, 1994.

A wordless book with startling pictures. It chronicles the flight of a bird through the skeleton of a large dinosaur. It also shows the bird flying back in time to when dinosaurs roamed the earth. (LP-UP)

Sattler, Helen Roney. *Baby Dinosaurs.* New York: Lothrop, Lee & Shepard, 1984.

Baby dinosaurs were born in many different sizes. Many of the remains of dinosaurs were found in nests. Dinosaurs were hatched from eggs. This book tells all about dinosaurs and how they grew up. (LP-UP)

Schlein, Miriam. *Before the Dinosaurs.* New York: Scholastic, 1996.

Was there life before dinosaurs? If so, what was it like? In this book, the reader learns about the first animal and plant life that preceded the dinosaurs. Also included is a time chart to show when they all appeared. (UP)

Simon, Seymour. *New Questions and Answers About Dinosaurs.* New York: Morrow Junior Books, 1990.

This book answers the most commonly asked questions about dinosaurs. Included in the book is an easy-to-use index to give readers access to the information quickly. Also, the drawings of the different dinosaurs are placed on a time line to show when the dinosaurs lived. (LP-UP)

Wood, A. J. *A Night in the Dinosaur Graveyard.* New York: Harper Festival, 1994.

A fictional book about Lucy and Max, who go on a fossil hunt with their grandfather, the Professor. While they are camping in a cave, strange things begin to happen. The book contains ten holograms so the reader can see what the dinosaurs looked like. (LP-UP)

Wheeling Across the Curriculum

Art

- Have children get into groups of three and create a dinosaur. One can make a head, one a body, and one a tail. These can be put together to create a "new" dinosaur. (LP-UP)
- Children can create their own dinosaur with modeling clay. They can be painted and fired and then put in a diorama. (MP-UP)
- A dinosaur puppet can be made by children. A cardboard cylinder from a roll of bathroom tissue can be used for the body. (LP-UP)

Creative Writing

- Using dog biscuits shaped like bones, pretend they are dinosaur bones. Have children write a story about the bone and the dinosaur it came from. (MP-UP)
- Children can write a journal entry describing what their life would be like if they were a big dinosaur such as a Tyrannosaurus rex. (MP-UP)

Critical Thinking

- Have children participate in a debate about why the dinosaurs became extinct. (UP)
- After reading *Baby Dinosaurs* by Helen Roney Sattler, children can play a matching game, matching baby dinosaur pictures with the adult dinosaur pictures. (MP-UP)
- After reading *If the Dinosaurs Came Back* by Bernard Most, children can brainstorm ideas of what they would do if dinosaurs were here on earth. LP-UP)

Critical Thinking/Science

- Children can do a classification activity showing dinosaurs with similar characteristics, such as being a plant eater or flying. (LP-UP)

Language Arts

- After reading one of the dinosaur alphabet books, children can make their own dinosaur alphabet book. (LP)
- After reading *Dinosaur's Thanksgiving* by Liza Donnally, children can plan a party to which they invite dinosaurs. (LP-UP)

Language Arts/Science

- Research can be done on the early scientists who first discovered the dinosaur fossils and the bones. Then students can write reports based on their research. (UP)

Mathematics

- Children can make charts comparing dinosaurs by size and weight. This chart can be used for other activities as well. (LP-UP)
- Math problems can be generated from the comparison chart previously mentioned. Math problems could be about size and weight of dinosaurs. (LP-UP)

Science

- Children can make a time line showing the three major periods when the dinosaurs lived on the earth. (UP)

Science/Art

- Children can add drawings of dinosaurs to the time line showing when they lived. (UP)
- Children can make a large mural showing different types of dinosaurs in their various habitats. (LP-UP)

Science/Writing

- Research can be done by children about the different types of dinosaurs. The research can be used to make a class book or individual book about dinosaurs. (MP-UP)

Dinosaur Research

Science (MP-UP)

Directions: In the box below, draw a picture of the dinosaur you learned about.

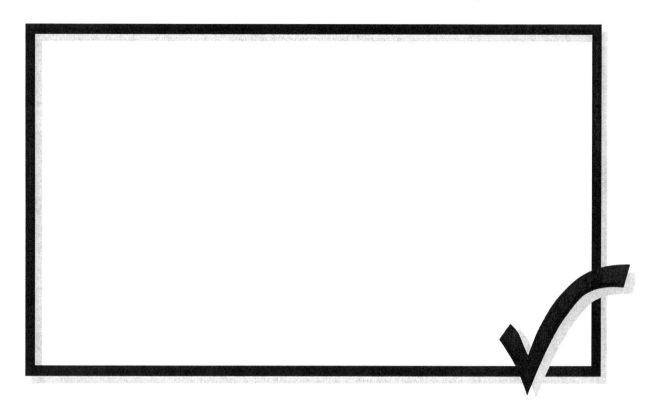

On the lines below write four facts you learned about the dinosaur in your picture.

1. _____

_____

2. _____

_____

3. _____

_____

4. _____

_____

Digging Up Bones

Language Arts (LP-UP)

Look at this dinosaur bone. What did the dinosaur look like?

Directions: Pretend you dug up the dinosaur bone. Write a story about where the bone came from and what the dinosaur looked like. Be creative in writing your stories.

Dinosaurs Roamed

Science (UP)

Directions: Make a chart showing when dinosaurs were on the earth. On the left side draw a picture of the dinosaur; on the right side write the period or dates when the dinosaur roamed the earth.

What is it that attracts children to dogs, and dogs to children? Whether they are a friend, guardian, playmate, or companion, dogs are perennial favorites with children. Explore, enrich, and exploit this attraction as you present this collection of dog books.

The books featured in this section encompass the many aspects of dog behavior—the good, the bad, and the comical.

A Rolling Start

Choose the Reading Rainbow video *The Adventures of Taxi Dog,* based on the book by Sal and Debra Barracca, to introduce this theme.

1. Construct "My Favorite Dog" bulletin board.

2. Have the children bring pictures of their favorite dogs. These can be photographs, hand-drawn pictures, or pictures cut from magazines. Place these pictures on a bulletin board. Ask each child to introduce his or her favorite dog to the class.

3. Create a canine vocabulary. Brainstorm with the children to create a list of words that they would use in talking about dogs. Encourage words that fall into the categories of physical description, behavior, necessary equipment, and breeds of dogs.

4. Make a list of these words and place them on the bulletin board for use in activities across the curriculum.

Booktalks

Auch, Mary Jane. *Bird Dogs Can't Fly.* New York: Holiday House, 1993.

Have you ever heard of a bird dog? Do you know what they are trained to do? This is a story about a bird dog, Blue, who does not do what he is supposed to do. When his master takes him hunting for birds, he does not bring the bird back to his master. He does not like to carry birds in his mouth. One day, his master shoots a goose and sends Blue to retrieve it. Blue finds the goose, only to discover that it is still alive, wounded, and unable to fly. Blue decides to leave the goose where it is and returns to his master without the goose.

Blue's master is very angry. That night Blue is sent to the barn without any supper. That is the night Blue decides to run away. Blue finds the wounded goose, and together they begin their journey south.

Since Goose has always flown south in the fall to escape the cold of the north, she thought it was not far. But as Blue and Goose travel by foot through cold and snow, they realize that getting to the south will be no easy task. As they travel, Goose walks along with Blue day after dreary day. One day Goose discovers her wing has healed and she can now fly. This is a time of decision. Will Goose abandon Blue and fly south to escape the cold? To read about the further adventures of Blue and to find out Goose's decision, check out *Bird Dogs Can't Fly.* (MP-UP)

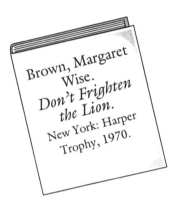

Brown, Margaret Wise. *Don't Frighten the Lion.* New York: Harper Trophy, 1970.

Can dogs go to the zoo? Have you ever seen a dog at the zoo? Think about it, because once there was a dog that lived by a zoo. At night the dog could hear the sounds that came from the zoo. This dog was very, very curious. It wanted to see for itself what these animals making the sounds looked like.

The dog's master decided that the dog should visit the zoo, and one afternoon he took the dog there. However, when the dog and his master arrived at the zoo gate, there was a big sign that read (pause and let the children predict what the sign read): NO DOGS. The zookeeper explained that the sight of a dog would scare the animals, especially the lion. Disappointed, the master and the dog went home. The next day the dog's master decided that he would dress the dog as a little girl. They bought a dress, socks, shoes, a hat, gloves, and even sunglasses. The dog learned to walk on its hind legs. When they went to the zoo the next day, the zoomaster, thinking the dog was a little girl, allowed them to pass into the zoo. Do the dog and his master get away with this trick? Are the animals fooled? You won't have to guess if you read this book to see what really happens. Read *Don't Frighten the Lion* by Margaret Wise Brown. (LP-MP)

Erickson, John R. *The Further Adventures of Hank, the Cowdog.* Houston: Gulf Publishing, 1988. (Available in Spanish.)

How many of you like stories about cowboys, ranches, and the West? I bet you all do. This is a yarn about an old dog named Hank and his friend, Drover. Hank is a very smart dog, and he's in charge of keeping the ranch secure. Hank prides himself on keeping the animals of the ranch safe. He thinks of Drover, another ranch dog, as slow-witted and bumbling. But things get turned around when a dead chicken is found on the ranch and Hank is the chief suspect. Hank has no choice but to leave the ranch. Drover is given Hank's job. In his misery Hank joins the hated coyotes.

One night Hank returns to the ranch with this scroungy bunch of coyotes and their leader, Scraunch. They are making a raid on the chicken house when they encounter Drover. What do you think will happen when the two former friends meet? [Pause for the children's responses.] Scraunch is really in a frenzy when they get to the chickens. He is shouting, "Kill, kill." Does Hank listen to Scraunch? Or does he go back to being a protector of the ranch animals? Is he on Scraunch's side or Drover's?

Read *The Further Adventures of Hank, the Cowdog,* to find out what happens to Hank and Drover. If you like this tale, then there are many other books about Hank, the Cowdog, you will enjoy. Keep readin', pardner! (UP)*

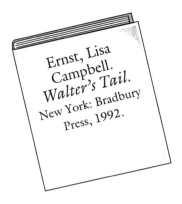

Ernst, Lisa Campbell. *Walter's Tail.* New York: Bradbury Press, 1992.

How many of you have ever stood next to a dog with a long, long tail? What happens when that dog starts wagging his tail? What happens in *Walter's Tail* is really the story of an old woman, Mrs. Tully, the dog, Walter, and the town folk.

Mrs. Tully lived alone in the house on the hill until she got Walter as a pup. She absolutely loved Walter at first sight. Mrs. Tully had never had a dog before. She thought Walter was the finest, most delightful dog, even after the first few "accidents" occurred.

The first of the accidents happened at home. This was an event hardly worth noting—Walter wagged his tail and broke a vase. It could happen to any pup, and Mrs. Tully could tell Walter was very sorry. However, as Walter grew larger so did his tail. Try as he might, he could not keep that tail from wagging. And so the accidents grew bigger and more serious. When Mrs. Tully and Walter went into town, all of Mrs. Tully's friends went the other way. The shopkeepers would put up their CLOSED signs when they saw Mrs. Tully and Walter coming down the street. Mrs. Tully and Walter felt very bad.

Should Mrs. Tully give Walter away? How can she get Walter to stop the tail from wagging? Do you have any ideas? [Pause to let the children respond.] One day Mrs. Tully and Walter did not go into town. Soon the townspeople were in a tizzy. Where were they? What had happened to them? To find out, be sure to read *Walter's Tail* by Lisa Campbell Ernst. You're sure to love Walter, even with his tail. (MP)

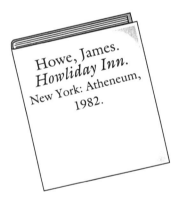

Howe, James. *Howliday Inn.* New York: Atheneum, 1982.

What's a family to do when they can't take their pets with them on vacation? Harold is a dog, big and lovable. Chester is a cat, worldly and smart. When their family goes on vacation and can't take their pets, Harold and Chester wind up at Chateau BowWow, otherwise known as Howliday Inn.

Harold and Chester are given bungalows for their stay. Harold likes his bungalow (translate that as cage). Harold likes his food dish, which has Doggie Din-din written on the bottom. Chester hates everything and thinks it is all too cutesy. He suspects everything is definitely not as it appears at the Howliday Inn. Chester is soon proven correct.

First, Louise, the poodle, disappears. Or did she just run away? Then Chester disappears, and Harold overhears that Chester was poisoned. What is really going on and who is responsible? Will Harold be able to find Chester and get to the bottom of all the mysterious happenings at the Howliday Inn? With the help of the other guests—Max, the bulldog, Violette, his friend, and Taxi, a wacky weird dog—Harold does piece together the answer to the puzzle. Read this suspenseful, entertaining book, *Howliday Inn.* (UP)*

Bibliography

Argueta, Manlio. *Magic Dogs of the Volcanoes,* or *Los Perros Magicos de los Volcanes.* San Francisco: Children's Book Press, 1990.

> For many years, the people living on the slopes of El Salvador's volcanoes were protected by magic creatures. They were the dogs called *cadejos.* One day Don Tonio and his 13 brothers decided to kill the magic dogs. They sent lead soldiers to find the dogs. But the volcanoes helped the *cadejos.* The volcanoes heated up and the lead soldiers melted down. Peace reigned once more on the slopes of El Salvador's volcanoes. (MP-UP)

Auch, Mary Jane. *Bird Dogs Can't Fly.* New York: Holiday House, 1993.

> Blue is a bird dog that hates to carry dead birds in his mouth. When he returns to his master after leaving a wounded goose in the pond, his master punishes Blue. Blue decides to run away. He locates the wounded goose and they start their journey south. (MP-UP)

Barracca, Debra and Sal Barracca. *Maxi, the Hero.* New York: Dial Books for Young Readers, 1991.

> Maxi, a dog, rides in the taxi of his owner, Jim. They spend their days giving people rides around the city. One day, something extraordinary happens, and Maxi becomes a hero. (MP-UP)
>
> Maxi, the taxi dog, is also featured in *The Adventures of Taxi Dog* and *A Taxi Dog Christmas.*

Brett, Jan. *First Dog.* New York: Harcourt, Brace, Jovanovich, 1988.

> This is a story of how Kip, the Cave Boy, escapes the many dangerous creatures of the Ice Age with the help of Paleo pup. In turn, Paleo pup becomes "First dog" when Kip makes him a special promise. (LP-UP)

Bridwell, Norman. *Clifford, the Big Red Dog.* New York: Scholastic, 1985.

> This is the first book of the Clifford series. Emily Elizabeth, the little girl who owns Clifford, introduces Clifford and tells all about him—faults and all. (LP-MP)

Brown, Marc. *Arthur's Pet Business.* Boston: Joy Street Books, 1990.

> In order to get a puppy of his own, Arthur must prove to his mother that he is responsible enough to take care of a dog. He does this by starting a pet-sitting business. (MP)

Brown, Margaret Wise. *Don't Frighten the Lion.* New York: Harper Trophy, 1970.

> A poodle who lives close to a zoo becomes very curious about the animals in the zoo. He asks his owner to take him there. But no dogs are allowed in the zoo. Little girls *are* allowed. So the poodle masquerades as a little girl in order to visit the zoo. (LP-MP)

Calhoun, Mary. *High Wire Henry.* New York: Morrow Junior Books, 1991.

> Henry, a cat, is feeling a bit jealous when the new puppy, Buttons, arrives. Then Buttons finds himself in a very dangerous spot. Henry turns out to be the high-wire hero. (MP-UP)

Cleary, Beverly. *Ribsy.* New York: Morrow Junior Books, 1964.

> Ribsy, Henry Higgins's dog, is sitting in the car when a very yappy pomeranian annoys him. He gets so excited that he scratches at the window of the car. Then he hits the automatic window opener. Ribsy flies through the window and into great adventure. (UP)*

Cleary, Beverly. *Strider.* New York: Morrow Junior Books, 1991.

> Leigh, the boy from the book *Dear Mr. Henshaw,* is writing in his diary again. This time he finds a dog on the beach, and he keeps a diary of his adventures. (UP)*

Cole, Joanna. *My Puppy Is Born.* New York: Morrow, 1973.

> The story of the birth of a litter of puppies is photographically recorded to show the pregnant mother, the pups being born, the nursing process, and the pup gaining its independence. (UP)

Day, Alexandria. *Carl's Afternoon in the Park*. New York: Farrar, Straus & Giroux. 1991.

This is a wordless book that, through its rich illustrations, takes us on a tour of the large city park. Sharing the adventure in the park are Carl, a rottweiler, and a baby. (LP)

Day, Alexandria. *Carl's Masquerade*. New York: Farrar, Straus & Giroux, 1992.

Carl, the rottweiler, and the baby follow the baby's parents to an outlandish costume party. Once again, the illustrations tell the story. (LP)

Emert, Phyllis Raybin. Working Dog Series. Howard Schroeder, ed. New York: Crestwood House, 1985.

This series on working dogs profiles the history of the work, the breed of dog, the types of training the dog receives, and the actual work the dogs do. Some titles in the series are listed here. (UP)

> *Guide Dogs*
> *Hearing Ear Dogs*
> *Law Enforcement Dogs*
> *Military Dogs*
> *Search and Rescue Dogs*
> *Sled Dogs*
> *Stunt Dogs*
> *Watch/Guard Dogs*

Erickson, John R. *The Further Adventures of Hank, the Cowdog*. Houston: Gulf Publishing, 1988.

When Hank becomes a suspect in a crime committed while he is in charge of the ranch's security, another adventure begins. This time Hank also goes down the wrong trail by joining a band of coyotes. But all is saved in the end. Hank the cowdog is featured in a series of adventure books, many available in Spanish. (UP)*

Ernst, Lisa Campbell. *Ginger Jumps*. New York: Bradbury Press, 1990.

Ginger, a circus dog, dreams about a little girl that would love her and take care of her. A clown and high jump help Ginger's dream come true. (LP-MP)

Ernst, Lisa Campbell. *Walter's Tail*. New York: Bradbury Press, 1992.

This is the story of a town, Mrs. Tully, and her wonderful dog Walter and his not-so-wonderful tail.(MP)

Evans, Mark. *Puppy*. New York: Dorling Kindersley. 1992.

This book covers *all* aspects of caring for a dog. It also includes sections on breeds of dogs and how to choose a dog. Written in easy-to-understand language, it is part of the American Society for Prevention of Cruelty to Animals series of Pet Care Guide for Kids. (UP)

Flack, Marjorie. *Angus and the Ducks*. New York: Doubleday, 1930.

Angus, the classic Scottie, goes for a walk and meets two ducks in the park. He enjoys scaring them with his big WOOF, but then the tables are turned. (LP-MP)

Flack, Marjorie. *Angus Lost*. New York: Doubleday, 1932.

Angus, a Scottish terrier, is a perennial favorite. In this story Angus goes exploring a little too far from home and meets a variety of creatures on his way back home. (LP-MP)

Gackenbach, Dick. *Claude Has a Picnic*. New York: Clarion Books, 1993.

Not only does Claude, the dog, engineer a neighborhood picnic, but he replaces the summer doldrums with fun for all. Claude is a very clever dog. (MP)

Gackenbach, Dick. *What's Claude Doing?* New York: Clarion Books, 1984.

Claude, the dog, is usually ready to go play whenever anyone asks. But one snowy day he confuses his friends by refusing to leave the house—he even refuses to chase cats. Read the book to find out the reason for this unusual behavior. (MP)

Hill, Eric. *Spot Goes to a Costume Party*. New York: G. P. Putnam's Sons, 1991.

An easy-to-read book that has lift-up flaps on every page. The animals are at a costume party; lifting the flaps reveal the animals having a great time. The Spot series includes holiday books such as *Spot's First Christmas* and *Spot's First Easter*. (LP)

Howe, James. *Howliday Inn.* New York: Atheneum, 1982.

 Harold, the dog, and Chester, the cat, are boarded at a place called Chateau BowWow while their family goes on vacation. Harold and Chester soon call it the Howliday Inn and get involved in the mysterious goings-on there. This is a lighthearted introduction to mysteries. (UP)*

Kellogg, Steven. *A Rose for Pinkerton.* New York: Dial Books for Young Readers, 1981.

 Everyone's favorite Great Dane, Pinkerton, has trouble adjusting when Rose, a kitten, joins the household. Pinkerton and Rose work it all out in a very entertaining manner. Pinkerton's adventures are featured in other Pinkerton Books. (MP)

Rand, Gloria. *Salty Dog.* New York: Henry Holt, 1989.

 This is the story of a puppy, Salty, and his owner, Zack. As Salty grows, so does the sailboat that Zack is building. By the time the sailboat is completed, Salty has learned about boats and going to sea. (MP)

Reiser, Lynn. *Any Kind of Dog.* New York: Greenwillow Books, 1992.

 Richard wants a dog—any kind of dog—but his mother thinks it would be too much trouble. She tries giving Richard other types of pets before Richard ends up with—any kind of dog. (MP)

Rockwell, Anne. *When Hugo Went to School.* New York: Macmillan, 1990.

 One day Hugo, the dog, follows the children to school. The principal puts him outside and finally calls the police to take Hugo away. It all ends well in this simply told story of Hugo's adventure at school. (LP)

Rylant, Cynthia. *Henry and Mudge in the Green Time.* New York: Bradbury Press, 1987.

 Three stories of the adventures of Henry and his dog, Mudge. An easy reader, this book is part of the Henry and Mudge Series. (LP-MP)

Zion, Gene. *Harry, the Dirty Dog.* New York: Harper & Row, 1956.

 Is Harry a white dog with black dots or just an all-black dog? It's hard to tell because Harry hides the scrub brush and runs off to get dirty. When he returns, his family doesn't recognize him. Harry realizes his mistake, digs up the scrub brush, and begs for a bath. Other "Harry" books are *No Roses for Harry, Harry by the Sea,* and *Harry and the Lady Next Door.* (MP)

Wheeling Across the Curriculum

Art

- Have the children use the letters from their favorite breed of dog's name and make a design. For example, a dalmation would go with black-and-white spots. (MP)

- Scan some dog pictures into the scrapbook on your computer. Demonstrate how to manipulate the pictures by cutting and pasting and adding features. (LP-UP)

- Do a short study of architectural detail. Ask the children to design a doghouse incorporating one architectural detail. (UP)

- Use finger paint to have children draw a dog. (LP)

Language Arts

- Model how to construct a riddle, using the following pattern:

    Describe the dog (size, color, fur, etc.).

    Give the characteristics of the dog.

    Ask "Who am I?"

    Example: "I am a very small dog. I am named after a state in Mexico. Who am I? A Chihuahua." (UP)

- Ask the children to sit in a circle. Have each child add a descriptive word to a stem sentence. Example: "See the dog. See the spotted dog. See the funny spotted dog." (LP)

- Everyone loves the Clifford books. Ask the children to work in pairs to write a story entitled "If We Owned Clifford for a Day." (MP-UP)

Mathematics

- Ask the children to make counting books using the pattern "My Dog Has . . ." (LP-MP)

- One dog year equals seven human years. Have the children figure out the age of a dog in human years at 2, 4, 7, and 12. (UP)

- Collect data on pet ownership from the children. Then graph how many children have dogs, cats, fish, birds, other pets, or no pets. (LP-UP)

Reading

- Compare the book *What's Claude Doing?* by Dick Gackenbach and any of the books from the Working Dog series by Phyllis Raybin Emert.

- Have the children list the differences and similarities between the books.

- Define the terms *fiction* and *nonfiction* for the children. Have them work in groups to sort a stack of books into fiction and nonfiction books. (MP-UP)

Science

- Read *First Dog* by Jan Brett. Use this book to help the children understand prehistoric times. (MP-UP)

- Brainstorm with the children to list facts about dogs. Use the "Favorite Dog" bulletin board as a launching point. List these facts under the words "ALL" and "SOME." For example, "ALL dogs have ears." "SOME dogs run very fast." (LP)

- Place the children in teams and have them go on a scavenger hunt for facts about dogs. Ask them to find the life expectancy of large dogs versus small dogs, a dog's body temperature, its respiration rate, the most popular breed, and so on. (UP)

Pet Sitting

Reading (LP-MP)

Directions: After reading *Arthur's Pet Business* by Marc Brown, pretend you are going to start a pet business. What kind of animals would you want to take care of? Make a poster advertising your new business.

"Collar" Those Reports

Reading (MP-UP)

Directions: Below you see five collars. When you read a book about dogs, keep track of the books you like by printing the title and author on the collar.

☐ ☐ Author _____

Title _____

☐ ☐ Author _____

Title _____

☐ ☐ Author _____

Title _____

☐ ☐ Author _____

Title _____

☐ ☐ Author _____

Title _____

Dog Care

Social Studies (MP-UP)

Directions: After you have read at least three books about dogs, list the book titles and then write your rules for taking care of a dog.

Books I've Read

Title: _____

Title: _____

Title: _____

My Rules for Dog Care

1.
_____

2.
_____

3.
_____

4.
_____

5.
_____

CHAPTER 6

FROM MAGIC TO MYSTERY: FAIRY AND FOLKTALES

The books found in this genre are called traditional literature, which includes all those stories that have been passed down from generation to generation. In earlier times, these were the stories told in the oral tradition. The reader can choose from the timeless fairy tales that contain the beautiful princess and a hero, usually in the form of a prince, or from the fables that teach a moral to the young. For the curious, there are the *pourquoi tales* that answer the question why. The tall tales are about those folk heroes from the American frontier who grew larger than life as people moved West. Also included in this genre are Native American myths and legends, which give insights into these cultures.

The bibliography for this chapter contains a wide variety of books. It includes books from the many subcategories of traditional tales, with selections for everyone's interests.

A Rolling Start

1. To introduce this genre to the children, give them samples of the different types of books that fit under the umbrella of traditional literature. Book jackets could also be put up on a bulletin board.

2. Have children make up characters that are larger than life and develop their own heroes like Paul Bunyan. The characters can be drawn on paper, cut out, and displayed around the room.

3. Have children brainstorm lists of the books that fit into each category of this genre. As the children read more traditional literature, they can add to the lists posted around the room.

Booktalks

Baumann, Hans. *Thank You, Brother Bear* (Original title: *Chip Has Many Brothers*). New York: Philomel, 1985.

As many folktales do, this one starts long ago and takes place in the far, frozen, cold north. Chip had two older brothers, Shining Spear and Strong Bow, who were mighty hunters. Chip loved the animals of the forest. He couldn't bring himself to harm them, even for food. Shining Spear and Strong Bow were going to hunt for their winter supply of food. They left Chip with his sister, Bright Sun, and their Grandmother, Nuni, and told him to take care of them. Not long after the hunters left, Bright Sun became ill. Nuni said she needed medicine that only Wise

Raven had. Chip was too young to go, but he decided to try anyway. Bright Sun needed the medicine.

After Chip started on his journey, he ran into many hardships. With each challenge, his friends of the forest came to help him. With their help, he was able to overcome the hardships and reach the home of Wise Raven. Wise Raven gave him the medicine. He took it back to help Bright Sun get better. Each time one of his brother animals helped him along his way, Chip would thank the animal.

When his two brothers returned from their hunt, the animals were there with Chip. The brothers asked why the animals were there. Grandmother Nuni said, "They are here because they are your brothers too and they helped Bright Sun."

To find out how the animals helped Chip and his family, read *Thank You, Brother Bear* by Hans Baumann. (LP-UP)

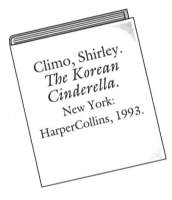

Climo, Shirley. *The Korean Cinderella*. New York: HarperCollins, 1993.

Long ago there were magical beings and spirits living in Korea. During this time, a daughter was finally born to an old couple. They named her Pear Blossom because her father planted a pear tree to celebrate her birth. The child grew each day and was very beautiful. One unhappy day, her mother died. Her father felt she needed a mother, so he went to the matchmaker to find himself a wife to help raise her. But Pear Blossom's father married a widow who did not treat her well. She made Pear Blossom work hard and was mean to her.

The years went on and things got worse. But Pear Blossom continued to get more beautiful. One day, the village was having a festival. Pear Blossom's stepmother gave her so much work she didn't think she would be able to go to the village.

The family left for the festival. Pear Blossom went to the field to do her work. As she worked in the field, the animals came to help her. What will happen? Will Pear Blossom finish in time to go to the festival? To find out what happens to Pear Blossom, read *The Korean Cinderella* by Shirley Climo. (LP-UP)

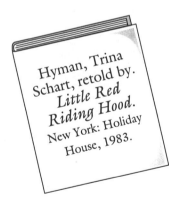

Hyman, Trina Schart, retold by. *Little Red Riding Hood*. New York: Holiday House, 1983.

As with all good stories, this one begins, once upon a time there was a little girl named Elisabeth who lived with her mother. One day her grandmother made her a cloak of red velvet. It was beautiful, and she wore it all the time. After that, people called Elisabeth Little Red Riding Hood.

One day Little Red Riding Hood's mother asked her to take a loaf of bread to her grandmother. To do this, she had to go through a forest. Her mother told her to be careful. As she went through the forest, she met a wolf. He asked her where she was going.

Now the wolf was sly. He decided to beat Little Red Riding Hood to her Grandmother's house. He took a shortcut through the forest and got there first.

What will happen to Little Red Riding Hood? What will the wolf do? Will something happen to Grandmother? To find out what happens to Little Red Riding Hood and her Grandmother, read Trina Schart Hyman's story. (LP-UP)

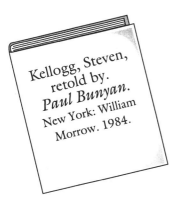

Kellogg, Steven, retold by. *Paul Bunyan.* New York: William Morrow. 1984.

From the time Paul Bunyan was a baby, he was big and strong. He pulled up the neighbor's trees and loaded them in the family's lumber wagon when he was a baby.

One day when he was a little older, he woke up to a world frozen under a layer of snow. In the snow was an ox calf. Paul rescued the calf from the ice and named her Babe, the blue ox, because she had turned that color from the cold. Babe remained blue throughout her life.

Paul and Babe both kept growing and growing until they were both huge! The Maine countryside where they lived became crowded, so Paul and Babe headed West. Together they worked in the lumber country as they moved West.

There are many tales about the things Paul Bunyan did. There are stories about him digging the St. Lawrence River and the Great Lakes. As he was crossing the desert, his big ax fell off his shoulder and made a deep cut in the ground. This cut is now known as the Grand Canyon. To find out more about Paul Bunyan, read the story by Steven Kellogg. (LP-UP)

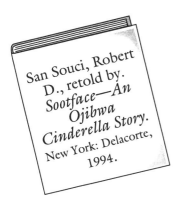

San Souci, Robert D., retold by. *Sootface—An Ojibwa Cinderella Story.* New York: Delacorte, 1994.

There are many Cinderella stories, including one by the Ojibwa tribe of the Great Lakes region. Sootface was the youngest of three daughters of a widow. The sisters were to share the work, but the older sisters were mean to the youngest one. They made her do all the work and cook all the meals. The fire singed her hair and burned her skin, making it rough. Because of this her sisters called her Sootface. Her sisters took the best fur and materials to make clothes for themselves. Because of this, there was nothing left for Sootface to wear.

Now, living on the other side of the lake was a great warrior with special powers. He could become invisible. One day he sent his sister across the lake to find him a wife. She was to find a maiden who was able to see him and look beyond his powers.

The warrior's sister asked all the young women the same questions: What does my brother look like and what is his bow made of? None of the young women could answer these questions. They didn't pass the test.

Sootface's two sisters decided to go visit the Invisible Being. They dressed in their finest clothes and set off. They met the Invisible Being's sister but couldn't answer her questions so they didn't get to see him.

Sootface prepared herself to go to the great warrior's lodge. As she walked through the village, her sisters and other village members made fun of her and called her names. Sootface ignored them all and kept going, setting out to find the lodge.

Will Sootface meet the Invisible Being's sister? Will she be able to answer the questions she asks? To find out if Sootface lives happily ever after, read *Sootface* by Robert D. San Souci. (MP-UP)

Bibliography

Andersen, Hans Christian. *The Steadfast Tin Soldier.* New York: HarperCollins, 1991.

One of Hans Christian Andersen's original tales, this is a holiday favorite. The one-legged soldier stands at attention with the other soldiers in the playroom. He admires the paper ballerina from afar. He wishes she knew how he felt. Many things happen to the tin soldier. But will he ever get to meet the ballerina? (LP-UP)

Baumann, Hans. *Thank You, Brother Bear* (Original title: *Chip Has Many Brothers*). New York: Philomel, 1985.

In the far north where it is very cold lived three brothers, their sister, and their grandmother. The oldest two brothers were great hunters, but Chip, the youngest, cared so strongly for the animals of the forest that he couldn't kill them. He would tell the animals when it was safe to come out. One day, the animals helped Chip solve a problem. (LP-UP)

Brothers Grimm. *Hansel and Gretel.* Saxonville, Mass.: Picture Book Studio, 1988. (Translated by Elizabeth D. Crawford.)

Once there was a woodcutter, his children, and his wife, who was their stepmother. They were very poor and had no food. The stepmother wanted to take the children to the forest and leave them. Hansel told his sister Gretel that he would save them. Hansel and Gretel must be brave when they go to the forest. (MP-UP)

Climo, Shirley, *The Korean Cinderella.* New York: HarperCollins, 1993.

A long time ago, there was a daughter born to an older couple. The day she was born her father planted a pear tree, so her mother called her Pear Blossom. The child grew into a beautiful young lady. Then her mother died, and her father decided to find another wife. What will happen when Pear Blossom gets a stepmother? (MP-UP)

Ernst, Lisa Campbell. *Little Red Riding Hood: A Newfangled Prairie Tale.* New York: Simon & Schuster Books for Young Readers, 1995.

There was a little girl who always wore a red-hooded sweatshirt when she rode her bike, so she was called Little Red Riding Hood. One day she volunteered to take some wheat-berry muffins to her grandma's house. As she was riding her bike, who should smell the wheat-berry muffins but a wolf? (LP-UP)

Hamilton, Virginia. *Her Stories—African American Folktales, Fairy Tales, and True Stories.* New York: Blue Sky Press, 1995.

This is a collection of stories about African American women. Some are based on folktales that have been passed down from generation to generation. Other stories may be true. All stories give the reader insights into the folktales that are part of American history. (MP-LP)

Heins, Paul, trans. *Snow White.* Boston: Little, Brown, 1974.

Once there was a Queen who wished for a child as white as the snow. The Queen died the day Snow White was born, and her father remarried a year later. Her stepmother was jealous of Snow White's beauty and commanded that she be taken into the forest. She escaped and went to live with the Seven Dwarfs. (LP-UP)

Hooks, William H. *Moss Gown.* New York: Clarion Books, 1987.

In the South lived a man and his three daughters. The two older daughters were mean to the younger one and sent her out of the house. As she wandered, she met a *gris-gris* (gree-gree) lady, who gave her a dress made of moss. She found help working in the kitchen of a plantation much like the one she grew up on. (MP-UP)

Huck, Charlotte. *Princess Furball.* New York: Mulberry, 1994.

Once upon a time there was a beautiful princess. Her father wanted her to marry an ogre. She asked for many gifts, thinking her father would never get all the gifts and she wouldn't have to marry the ogre. But her father found all the gifts. What will she do? (MP-UP)

Hyman, Trina Schart, retold by. *Little Red Riding Hood.* New York, Holiday House, 1983.

Little Red Riding Hood's real name is Elisabeth. She got her nickname because she would only wear the red cloak made by her grandmother. One day, as she was taking a basket of goodies to her grandmother, she ran into a wolf. What will happen to her? (LP-UP)

Isaacs, Anne. *Swamp Angel.* New York: Dutton Children's Books, 1994.

After Angelina Longrider was born, she grew rapidly. By the time she was two, she had built her first cabin. She continued to grow until she was very large. Many stories were told about her in Tennessee, such as how she helped the Smoky Mountains come to be. (LP-UP)

Johnston, Tony. *The Tale of Rabbit and Coyote.* New York: Scholastic, 1994.

There are many stories from the Southwest and Mexico that feature coyote as the trickster, the one always playing jokes and tricks. In this story from Mexico, the rabbit is always playing tricks on coyote. This makes coyote angry. Will coyote play a trick in return? This book includes a glossary of Spanish expressions. (MP-UP)

Kellogg, Steven, retold by. *Jack and the Beanstalk.* New York: Morrow Junior Books, 1991.

Jack lives with his widowed mother. They are poor, so she sends Jack to sell their cow. He meets a man who offers him beans for the cow. His mother is mad and throws the beans out the window. The beans grow, and Jack has an adventure. (LP-UP)

Kellogg, Steven. *Johnny Appleseed.* New York: Scholastic, 1988.

John Chapman was born September 26, 1774. He later went around the country planting apple trees. Many tall tales were made up about him, and he became known as Johnny Appleseed. (MP-UP)

Kellogg, Steven, retold by. *Mike Fink.* New York: Morrow Junior Books, 1992.

Back in the days when people were settling and moving into the frontier, there were many men who helped move goods and people along the frontier waterways. Mike Fink was King of the Keelboat Men. The stories and tall tales told about him were ones of fighting alligators and saving settlers. (MP-UP)

Kellogg, Steven, retold by. *Paul Bunyan.* New York: William Morrow, 1984.

Paul Bunyan was born in Maine. Some say he was the biggest and smartest baby ever born in the state. He grew so big that the stories about him became just as big—such as how he dug the Great Lakes or became the strongest lumberjack ever. (LP-UP)

Kellogg, Steven, retold by. *Pecos Bill.* New York: William Morrow, 1986.

When Pecos Bill was a baby, his family moved to Texas. As they were crossing the Pecos River, Bill fell out and landed in the river. He was saved by the coyotes and taken to live with them. As he grew, he became very strong and did many wild things. (LP-UP)

Kimmel, Eric A., retold by. *The Gingerbread Man.* New York: Holiday House, 1993.

An old woman and old man decided to bake some gingerbread men. When one of the men had cooled, they decorated him. Much to their surprise, he jumped off the table and ran away. On his journeys, the gingerbread man met many animals and had many adventures. (LP-UP)

Lester Julius. *John Henry.* New York: Dial Books for Young Readers, 1994.

There are many stories about John Henry and his life. On the day he was born, he jumped out of his mother's arms and began to grow. As an adult, he went to work on the railroad and drove steel to build the railroad through the mountain. (MP-UP)

McCarthy, Tara, ed. *Multicultural Fables and Fairy Tales*. New York: Scholastic, 1991.

This collection has short fables, fairy tales, legends, and why-stories from around the world. Also included are activities that children can do to help them become aware of stories from many cultures. (LP-UP)

Rosen, Michael. *How Giraffe Got Such a Long Neck . . . A Tale from East Africa*. New York: Trumpet, 1993.

Did you know that in the beginning the Giraffe had a short neck and looked more like a deer? This folktale from East Africa explains how it got its long neck. (LP-UP)

San Souci, Robert D., retold by. *Sootface— An Ojibwa Cinderella Story*. New York: Delacorte Press, 1994.

In this Ojibwa Cinderella story, Sootface lives with her two older sisters and widowed father. Her sisters are mean to her. They call her Sootface because cinders from the cooking fires have scarred her face and singed her hair. Sootface tries to find the Invisible Being who is looking for a wife. (MP-UP)

San Souci, Robert D. *The Talking Eggs*. New York: Dial Books for Young Readers, 1989.

There is a widow with two daughters, Rose and Blanche. They raise chickens and cotton to support themselves. The oldest daughter, Rose, is mean, but Blanche is kind and good. In the woods, Blanche finds an old lady who takes her home. Then strange things happen, and Blanche finds treasures. Rose tries to find the old lady because she wants the treasures too. (MP-UP)

Scieszka, Jon and Lane Smith. *The Stinky Cheese Man and Other Fairly Stupid Tales*. New York: Penguin Books, 1992.

This is a collection of old fairy tales told from a slightly different point of view. The book includes such stories as "Chicken Licken," "The Really Ugly Duckling," and "Jack's Bean Problem." (UP)

Steptoe, John. *Mufaro's Beautiful Daughters*. New York: Lothrop, Lee & Shepard, 1987.

A man named Mufaro had two daughters who were very beautiful. Manyara was always unhappy, but Nyasha was kind and gentle. It was announced that the king was going to have a ball to find a queen. The sisters wanted to go to the city to attend the ball. Many things happened to them as they went on their journey. (MP-UP)

Watson, Richard Jesse, retold by. *Tom Thumb*. San Diego: Harcourt Brace Jovanovich, 1989.

A long time ago, a man and a woman wanted children very badly. Finally, the woman had a baby, who was as long as her husband's thumb. Because he was so tiny, they named him Tom Thumb. His life was scary because he was so small, but this caused many adventures. He survived these perils to become a hero. (MP-UP)

Yolen, Jane. *Sleeping Ugly*. New York: Coward, McCann, & Geoghegan, 1981.

Princess Miserella was very beautiful, but on the inside she was mean and disagreeable. Plain Jane was liked by everyone and was kind to all. The Fairy Godmother put a spell on Princess Miserella, but an accident happened. What will happen to Jane and Miserella? (MP-UP)*

Young, Ed, trans. *Lon Po Po: A Red-Riding Hood Story from China*. New York: Philomel, 1989.

There was an old woman who lived in the country with her three children. It was their grandmother's birthday, so the mother left her daughters to go visit grandmother (called PoPo in Chinese). A wolf watched the mother leave and tried to fool the daughters. (LP-UP)

Wheeling Across the Curriculum

Art

- Using the characteristics of a hero, children can draw what a folk hero would look like to them. (LP-UP)

- After reading one of the Chinese fairy tales, children can learn about Chinese art and scrolls. (LP-UP)

- Children can illustrate their favorite character from one of the books. (LP-UP)

Art/Language Arts

- What does a wicked stepmother look like? Children can draw a picture of a wicked stepmother or make a list of words that describe a wicked stepmother. This activity can also be done for a good stepmother. (LP-UP)

Creative Writing

- Children can modify a fairy tale to fit the region where they live. For example, they could write a southern version of the *Three Little Pigs. (*MP-UP)

- Children can use their imaginations and rewrite the ending of one of the stories. (LP-UP)

- After learning about the characteristics of a fairy tale, children can write their own fairy tales. (LP-UP)

Critical Thinking

- Children can analyze the traits of the characters. For example, why was Sootface able to see the Invisible Being? (MP-UP)

- After they read a well-known tale such as *Little Red Riding Hood,* have children sequence the events of the story in the order they took place. (LP-UP)

- Children can write a essay about their reactions to any of the books/characters in this genre. (MP-UP)

- Children can list the characteristics that make a person larger than life. (MP-UP)

Language Arts/Comprehension

- All fairy tales have characters with magical powers or special traits. Children can classify and categorize these various traits. (MP-UP)

- The many *Cinderella* stories lend themselves to activities such as comparing and contrasting the setting, plot, theme, and characters. (MP-UP)

Mathematics

- After reading *Lon Po Po,* translated by Ed Young, children can learn about tangrams from China. (LP-UP)

Physical Education

- Children play different games in different cultures. These games can be researched and learned by the children. Chinese jump rope is an example of one such game. (LP-UP)

Science

- Many stories in this genre deal with the moon and stars. This can be a springboard to studying about the solar system. (LP-UP)

Social Studies

- After reading *Sootface* by Robert D. San Souci, children can do research to find out where the Ojibwa tribe lives. (MP-UP)

- Children can explore the different types of houses characters live in and why those houses are found in that particular area. (LP-UP)

- Food is a common theme in many of the books in this genre. Children can do research on the different types of foods, which can then be cooked and tasted by the children. (LP-UP)

- After reading the various *Cinderella* stories or other fairy tales, children can make maps to locate where all the stories take place. (LP-UP)

Behind the Wall

Critical Thinking/Creative Writing (LP-UP)

Who lives in the castle? What is in there?

Directions: What do you think is behind the castle wall? On the wall, write what you think is inside.

Magic Box

Science (MP-UP)

What is magic? How does it work?

Directions: Look up magic in the dictionary and encyclopedia. Inside the magic box, write down what you think magic is.

Who, What, When?

Language Arts (MP-UP)

Many traditional tales follow a sequential order of events, with the action focused on the main characters.

Directions: After reading a traditional tale such as *Cinderella*, fill out the time line. List the events that have taken place in the story. Across the time line, write the events in the order they happen. Assign a color to each character and underline the events that happened to him or her in that color. This will make it easier to tell what happens to whom.

Example:

(Events from *Cinderella*)

Father marries Stepmother	Cinderella cooks and cleans	
Cinderella's mother dies	Stepsisters make Cinderella work	Lives happily ever after

Story Title:

_____

Characters:

_____

_____

_____

Time Line:

_____

_____

CHAPTER 7

..⚐CREEPY CRAWLERS: INSECTS AND SPIDERS

This chapter is restricted to those six- and eight-legged creatures known as insects and spiders. Most children are either enamored of or repulsed by these creepy crawlers. It seems there is no neutral ground. In either case, children are attracted to the books that feature these creatures.

The books selected for this chapter include nonfiction books with wonderful photographs that will enrich your children's understanding of insects, as well as fictional books that present insects as the main or supporting characters. Have fun as you and the children explore the fascinating world of insects.

A Rolling Start

Patricia McKissack and Frederick McKissack's book *Bugs* is featured in the Reading Rainbow video of the same name. It is a great departure point for your journey into the world of insects and spiders.

1. After viewing the video, ask the children to name the essential parts of an insect.

2. Draw and label the three parts of an insect's body. Make it large enough so that the whole class can see it, or use a ready-made diagram, if available.

3. Point to the head, thorax, and abdomen, and label the corresponding parts. Count the six legs. If you wish to be very creative, have the legs precut and have the children attach them to the insect's body, making sure that all are attached to the thorax (the center section).

4. Have the children draw their own diagram of an ant's body (head, thorax, and abdomen) on white painting paper and color it very heavily with black crayon.

5. Have the children paint over the body parts with bright tempera paints. The black crayon will resist the paint and you'll have a roomful of ants on brightly colored backgrounds.

6. After the paint is dry, the children may want to add the legs and antennae cut from paper to give a three-dimensional effect.

Booktalks

Gibbons, Gail. *Spiders.* New York: Holiday House, 1993.

Did you know Little Miss Muffet, of nursery rhyme fame, was a real little girl? She lived about 200 years ago, and her father, a spider expert, made her eat mashed spiders to cure a cold. Did you know there are about 30,000 different types of spiders? They come in all colors and sizes. Did you know you can learn about a spider by looking at its web? Not all spiders build the same types of webs. What kind of spiderwebs have you seen? [Pause for responses.] Spiders build their webs to catch their food. Some spiders build funnel webs, some sheet webs, and others orb webs. Although almost all spiders spin webs, a few do not. An example of a spider that does not build a web is the wolf spider. It hides in the grass or under rocks, and when it sees "dinner" it runs out quickly and grabs its prey.

How many of you think that a spider could live under water? To find out whether there are spiders that live underwater—or many other facts about spiders—check out this easy-to-read book called *Spiders* by Gail Gibbons. (LP-MP)

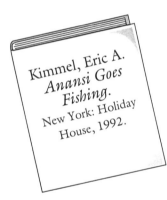

Kimmel, Eric A. *Anansi Goes Fishing.* New York: Holiday House, 1992.

Anansi is a spider who is featured in Ashanti folktales. He is a very lazy spider and is always looking for a way to get out of work. Do you know anyone who is like that? I think we all may have a little bit of Anansi in us. One day Anansi meets his friend, Turtle. Turtle is carrying a nice, big fish. Anansi asks turtle to teach him how to fish. Turtle knows Anansi well and knows that Anansi will try to trick him into doing all the work. Turtle tricks Anansi by giving him two choices:

Anansi can make a net or he can get tired.

Anansi absolutely does not want to get tired. So Turtle sits in a lawn chair "getting tired," while Anansi works hard making the net.

The next day Turtle once again tricks Anansi. This time Anansi chooses to set the net in the river rather than "get tired." So while Turtle relaxes, Anansi struggles to set the net.

Finally the fish is caught and cooked—by Anansi, of course—and the time comes to eat the fish. Once again, Turtle tricks the "lazy" spider.

If you want to know how all this trickery works out, you'll have to read *Anansi Goes Fishing* by Eric Kimmel. (UP)

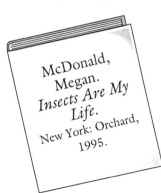

McDonald, Megan. *Insects Are My Life.* New York: Orchard, 1995.

What do you think the title, *Insects Are My Life*, means? Do you think that someone is exaggerating?

Meet Amanda, a little girl who is totally fascinated with insects. Let me give you some examples of just how much she loves insects. When her brother, Andrew, collects bugs in a jar, Amanda releases them. Amanda collects bugs, but she never collects living bugs. Hers are dead, and she keeps the shells. Amanda also collects bug bites. She has twenty-two on just one leg. Amanda turns on the light in her bedroom at night to attract bugs through her open window. I'd say she is totally dedicated to insects. Wouldn't you?

When Amanda goes to school, the kids find out about her love of insects. A boy named Victor really starts to tease her. He calls her "four eyes" and "bug eyes." Amanda replies that she has compound eyes.

When Victor and Amanda get into a loud argument at school, the teacher makes Amanda sit in a chair facing the wall. Amanda gets home from school that night and tells her mother she's not going back. When she does go back to school, Victor calls Amanda a cricket and Amanda calls Victor a worm. (A worm, of course, is not an insect.) And so it goes.

Will Amanda continue getting in trouble at school? How do you think this problem can be solved? To discover the solution to Amanda's problems, and to laugh along the way, read *Insects Are My Life* by Megan McDonald. (MP-UP)

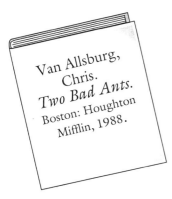

Van Allsburg, Chris. *Two Bad Ants.* Boston: Houghton Mifflin, 1988.

Do you know what a crystal is? Can you draw a picture of one? Picture a crystal small enough for a scout ant to carry. What crystal could be that small? And what small crystal tastes so-o-o good? Can you guess what this crystal is? [Pause for responses.] It's sugar. You know how ants love sugar. When the scout ant brings the sugar to the ant colony, the queen ant takes one taste and sends the worker ants for more crystals. The line of ants go through the grass, up the wall of the house, and over the window ledge. They troop into the kitchen and the sugar bowl. Each ant picks up a single crystal of sugar and starts the journey back to the ant colony. All but two ants.

These two ants decide to stay and eat the crystals right there. They eat so much sugar that they get very, very full and fall asleep. The next morning their whole world turns upside down. A huge scoop plucks them from the crystals and plunges them into a boiling brown lake. Can you guess what is really happening?

Read about the rest of the adventures of these *Two Bad Ants* and enjoy the ant's view of the world as drawn by Chris Van Allsburg. (MP-UP)

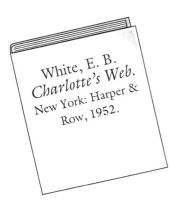

White, E. B. *Charlotte's Web.* New York: Harper & Row, 1952.

What would you do for your best friend if you knew he was going to die? I know you'd try to prevent his death. That's the situation in *Charlotte's Web.* But let me begin at the beginning.

Wilbur is the runt—that means the smallest—of a litter of pigs. The farmer is about to slaughter Wilbur. But Fern, the farmer's daughter, begs for Wilbur's life. She is given this runt to raise. When Wilbur reaches a certain size, he is sold to a farmer down the road, Fern's Uncle Zuckerman. Wilbur's new home has many barnyard characters such as a goose, a lamb, a rat named Templeton, and finally Charlotte, the spider.

One day the ram lets Wilbur know that in the fall, Wilbur will become pork chops. Depressed, Wilbur spends most of the night crying. What a shocking thought it is to Wilbur that he is part of someone's food chain. Charlotte reassures Wilbur that she will devise a plan to save his life. You might think, "Now what can a tiny spider do?" But you haven't met Charlotte.

With reluctant assistance from Templeton, she does come up with a life-saving plan. You will have to read the book, *Charlotte's Web* by E. B. White, to see if the plan really works. (UP)*

Bibliography

Aylesworth, Jim. *Old Black Fly.* New York: Henry Holt, 1992.

A totally delightful and disgusting trip through the alphabet with an old black fly. It lands in the honey, naps on a quilt, and sniffs the salami. Yuck! It is chased from page to page with the refrain "Shoo fly! Shoo fly! Shoo." The letters of the alphabet are printed in color in each page's verse. (LP)

Brown, Margaret Wise. *The Grasshopper and the Ants.* New York: Disney Press, 1993.

The traditional story of the grasshopper and the ants is illustrated Disney-style. The grasshopper may have played while the ants worked, but even so, when the grasshopper shows up at the ants' place in the depths of winter, the queen of the ants allows him to stay. (MP)

Carle, Eric. *The Very Quiet Cricket.* New York: Philomel, 1990.

The very quiet cricket hops through the book receiving greetings from all the other insects, but when he rubs his wings together nothing happens. In the evening, he sees a lovely female cricket. This time he's not so quiet. (Most editions have a battery that makes a cricket sound at the end of the book.) (LP-MP) Other, similar books by Eric Carle are *The Grouchy Lady Bug, The Very Busy Spider, The Firefly,* and *A Very Hungry Caterpillar.* (LP-MP)

Gackenbach, Dick. *Little Bug.* New York: Clarion Books, 1981.

Little Bug is afraid of his world and hiding in a hole when a voice tells him of all the pleasures of life he is missing. Little Bug leaves the hole and discovers the risks and the joys of living. (LP)

Gibbons, Gail. *Spiders.* New York: Holiday House, 1993.

This easy-to-read book tells many facts about spiders, including the many types of spiders, the history of spiders, and the types of webs spiders spin. It contrasts a spider's body to that of an insect. The simple illustrations make it an attractive, understandable book for small children. (LP-MP)

Kimmel, Eric A., retold by. *Anansi Goes Fishing.* New York: Holiday House, 1992.

Anansi, a very lazy spider, meets his friend, Turtle, carrying a nice big fish. Anansi asks Turtle to teach him how to fish, and Turtle does exactly what the spider asks. Anansi thinks that he will trick the turtle, but things get quite turned around. This time the trickster is tricked.(UP)

Kirk, David. *Miss Spider's Tea Party.* New York: Scholastic, 1994.

This is a counting book (1–10) as well as a picture book. Miss Spider invites the insects, starting with two timid beetles, to tea. The insects all flee. Finally, one wet moth is forced to stay, and Miss Spider has her tea party. (LP-MP)

Kraus, Robert. *Spider's First Day at School.* New York: Scholastic, 1987.

Spider returns to school in the fall to discover that his teacher this year will be Miss Quito. All goes well, from the lessons to the football game. This is one of the Spider series of books. (MP)

McDonald, Megan. *Insects Are My Life.* New York: Orchard, 1995.

When Amanda says insects are her life, she means it. She finds that it can be very lonely, both at home and at school, to have a passion that no one else shares. Finally, her teacher sits her next to a little girl who, although not crazy about insects, finds reptiles to be fascinating. (MP-UP)

McKissack, Patricia and Frederick McKissack. *Bugs.* Chicago: Children's Press, 1988.

Colorful illustrations and easy-to-read text tell the story of a young girl and boy looking for bugs. They first find one bug and continue looking until they find five bugs. This book is useful for children beginning their reading and counting experiences. (LP)

Nathan, Cheryl. *Bugs and Beasties: ABC.* Boca Raton, Fla.: Cool Kids Press, 1995.
    A single bug or beastie is illustrated for each letter of the alphabet. There is a brief description of all the creatures featured at the end of the book. (LP)

Palotta, Jerry. *The Icky Bug Counting Book.* Watertown, Mass.: Charles Bridge Publishing, 1992.
    Starting with zero bugs on the first page, this book counts up to 25 blister beetles. Each page has interesting facts about "icky bugs." (LP-MP)

Polacco, Patricia. *The Bee Tree.* New York: Philomel, 1993.
    Mary Ellen is tired of reading. That's when Grandpa decides it's time to find the bee tree. As they search for the bee tree, the town joins them for the honey hunt. (MP-UP)

Poulet, Virginia. *Blue Bug Visits Mexico.* Chicago: Children's Press, 1990.
    This book from the Blue Bug series has Blue Bug discovering the arts, crafts, foods, and dances of Mexico. (LP)

Rounds, Glen. *I Know an Old Lady Who Swallowed a Fly.* New York: Holiday House, 1990.
    The familiar verse is given a light touch with the illustrations of Glen Rounds. The ending, however, remains the same: she swallowed a horse—she died, of course. (LP)

Rowan, James P. *Ants: Insects.* Vero Beach, Fla.: Rourke Corp., 1993.
    This book contains everything children would like to know about ants. It is easy to read and contains photographs, a glossary, and an index. (MP-UP)

Royston, Angela. *What's Inside? Insects.* New York: Dorling Kindersley, 1992.
    Various insects are depicted both photographically (their exteriors) and graphically (their internal organs). The photographs and illustrations are placed on opposite pages, and the illustrations look like the photographs of the insects with their shells peeled off. Fascinating information. (MP-UP)

Sardegna, Jill. *The Roly-Poly Spider.* New York: Scholastic, 1994.
    The Roly-Poly spider spins a fine web, and as the other insects "drop in," she proceeds to have breakfast, lunch, and dinner. As she gets rounder and rounder, misfortune befalls her, and she gets stuck in a drainpipe. (LP)

Souza, D. M. *What Bit Me? Creatures All Around Us.* Minneapolis: Carolrhoda Books, 1991.
    This small book is stuffed with information on biting, stinging, and poisonous insects. It contains photographs, a glossary, and an index. (UP)

Szekeres, Cyndy. *Ladybug, Ladybug, Where Are You?* New York: Golden Books, 1991.
    Two mice find a glass jar with their friend, Ladybug, on top of it. Although the mice find many insects to put into their jar, they cannot find Ladybug. However, if the reader looks closely, Ladybug is there on every page. (LP-MP)

Van Allsburg, Chris. *Two Bad Ants.* Boston: Houghton Mifflin, 1988.
    When a scout ant returns with news of the sparkling crystal it has found, the story of the two bad ants begins. The two ants' close encounters with becoming someone's breakfast and Chris Van Allsburg's illustrations from the ants' perspective combine to make this an unforgettable book. (MP-UP)

Watts, Barrie. *Dragonfly.* Englewood Cliffs, N.J.: Silver Burdett Press, 1988.
    The life cycle of a dragonfly is portrayed through line drawings and photographs. From the egg through the entire cycle, from underwater to on the surface, the whole story of the dragonfly is told. (MP-UP)

White, E. B. *Charlotte's Web.* New York: Harper & Row, 1952.
    This is a classic tale of friendship. Charlotte, a spider, becomes the very best friend of Wilbur, a pig destined for slaughter. In a very ingenious way, Charlotte selflessly saves Wilbur's life. This classic is worth presenting to children over and over again. (UP)*

Wolkstein, Diane. *Step by Step.* New York: Morrow Junior Books, 1994.
    Ant goes to spend the day with her friend, Grasshopper. They sip nectar from a flower, float on a leaf, and dance in the rain. Just before dark, Ant returns contentedly to her home. (LP)

Wheeling Across the Curriculum

Art

- To make a butterfly, have the children trace around a butterfly wing pattern placed on the fold of a piece of white paper. Next, have them cut out the pattern and paint the wings. Attach the painted butterfly to the end of a tongue depressor. (LP-UP)

- Give the children clay and pipe cleaners and have them create their own creepy crawler. (LP)

Dance

- After children observe the movements of insects, ask them to make their bodies move in the same manner. Put the movements to music. (LP)

Language Arts

- Direct the children to choose an insect, research it, and write a short report on the insect. (UP)

- Have the children share their reports but not announce what the insect is until the end of the report. (UP)

- Have the children write and illustrate a story from the spider's point of view. (UP)

- Have the children make charts listing "all spiders" and "some spiders" and direct the children to categorize their facts accordingly. (UP)

- Play rhyming games using a beanbag. Toss the beanbag and ask the child to give a rhyming word when he or she catches the beanbag. Use these words for your rhyming game: bug, head, bee, ant, grasshopper, cricket, leg, eye, fly, zig, buzz, hop. (LP)

- Catch the "Writing Bug." Have the children's stories displayed on a large spiderweb. (LP-UP)

Mathematics

- Use the insect counting books to practice counting. (LP)

- Play "Which Is Bigger?" An ant or a bee? A horsefly or a ladybug? A grasshopper or a cricket? A tarantula or a cockroach? (LP)

- Introduce the concepts of thirds by displaying the three parts of an insect—head, thorax, and abdomen. Remove one part and see what is left. (UP)

- Try the same activity to introduce sixths, using insects' legs. (UP)

Music

- Use Glen Rounds' book *I Know an Old Lady Who Swallowed a Fly* to introduce the song with the same title. Children can create movements to go with the verses of the song. (LP-UP)

- Listen to a tape of Rimsky-Korsakov's *Flight of the Bumblebee*. Ask the children to guess what insect inspired the music. (LP-UP)

- Ask the children to create a beat for various insects. Use the instruments in a rhythm band. (MP-UP)

Reading

- Give out "I'm Buggy over Books" certificates to children who read five or more books on insects. (LP-UP)

- Make periodicals that have articles on insects and spiders available to the children. Use *Ranger Rick, Zoobooks,* or *Ladybug* magazines. (UP)

- Post insect riddles weekly and see who comes up with the correct answer. Offer a small prize (sticker, bookmark) for correct answers. *Buggy Riddles* by Katy Hall is a great source of riddles. (MP-UP)

Science

- Tack up butcher paper for a mural entitled "Where do they live?" Have the children paint in the homes of ants, bees, spiders, and butterflies. (LP-UP)

- Mark off a square yard of grass in various areas and have the children observe and record any sightings of insects in that area. (LP-UP)

- Use Eric Carle's book *A Very Hungry Caterpillar* to follow the metamorphosis of a caterpillar. If possible, purchase cocoons from a science supply store. (LP-UP)

- Direct the children to fold a paper into fourths. On each quarter, have the children draw a picture of an egg, larvae, cocoon, and butterfly. Cut along the fold lines and hang the quarters from a coat hanger to display. (MP-UP)

Creepy Crawlers in ABC Order

Language Arts (MP-UP)

Directions: Arrange these words in alphabetical order.

1. Dragonfly   1. _____

2. Housefly   2. _____

3. Bee   3. _____

4. Caterpillar   4. _____

5. Grasshopper   5. _____

6. Swallowtail   6. _____

7. Firefly   7. _____

8. Spider   8. _____

9. Tarantula   9. _____

10. Mosquito   10. _____

Directions: Unscramble the insect names below.

Etleeb_____   fburttyle_____   cketcri_____   spaw_____

Favorite Creepy Crawlies Books

Reading (MP-UP)

Directions: List the author and title for your three favorite Creepy Crawlie books.

Author:_____

Title:_____

Author:_____

Title:_____

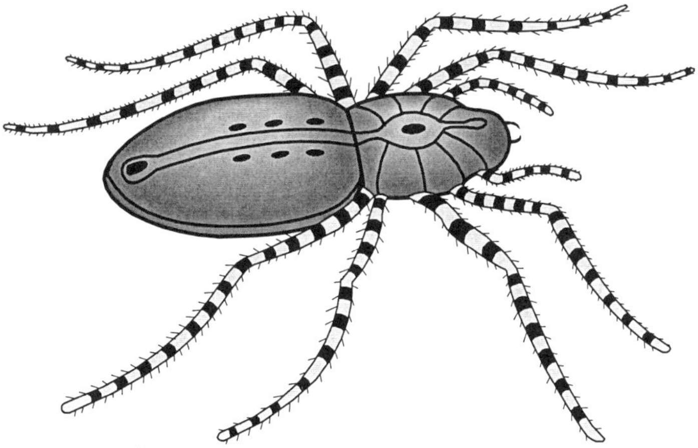

Author:_____

Title:_____

Where Do I Live?

Science (LP-UP)

Directions: Draw a home for the bee, the ant, and the spider.

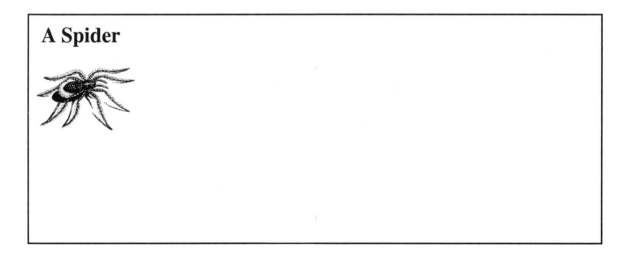

From Mickey Mouse to Mighty Mouse, mice have always intrigued children. Mice are portrayed as sympathetic characters, always having to outwit the big, mean tomcats. Mice use their wits to survive and rarely threaten anyone. The small conquers the mighty, and therein may lie the appeal to children.

A Rolling Start

Show the children the Reading Rainbow videotape *If You Give a Mouse a Cookie,* which uses the book by Laura Joffe Numeroff.

1. Have the children list the sequence of events as they occur in the video, using if-then statements.

2. Write the statements on butcher paper.

3. Brainstorm with the children to come up with other titles for books patterned after this title. Example: If you give a lion a lollipop . . . or, if you give a tiger a tickle . . . The children will quickly catch on and probably be ahead of you with their if-then statements. If you want the children to take their titles to the next step, have them come up with the "then" part of their sentence. Example: If you give a lion a lollipop, then he may get it stuck in his mane, and if it gets stuck in his mane, then . . . This activity can be done with a large group of children or in a small circle. It is a great oral language development activity.

Booktalks

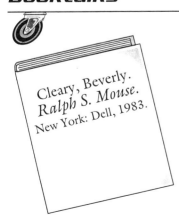

Cleary, Beverly.
Ralph S. Mouse.
New York: Dell, 1983.

What do you do when *you* see a mouse? Have you ever had a mouse in your classroom? If you have, I can guarantee you it was nothing like Ralph S. (for Smart) Mouse. Ralph has learned to talk by listening to TV and the conversations of children. His friend is Ryan, a boy who lives at the Inn with Ralph. Not only does Ralph talk, but he also rides a motorcycle.

When there are problems at the Inn, Ralph talks Ryan into taking him to his fifth-grade class at Irwin J. Sneed Elementary School. The adventure begins.

Ralph becomes a class project, the subject of a newspaper article, and the cause of a fight between Ryan and a boy named Brad. In this fight, Ralph's motorcycle is broken.

The experiment of taking Ralph to school leaves everyone—Ralph, Ryan, and Brad—unhappy. To find out how this all works out, read *Ralph S. Mouse* by Beverly Cleary. (UP)*

Dubanevich, Arlene. *Tom's Tail*. New York: Viking, 1990.

How do you think mice would behave if the house cat just slept? Do you think they'd stay in their mouse holes? No, they would not. As Tom, the house cat, got lazier and lazier, he slept more and more. At first the mice were cautious as they came out to play. They tiptoed around Tom. Then they played in front of him. Finally they even called him names, such as "fish breath." Did Tom open even one eye? No, Tom just slept and slept. He slept until one day the mice decided to swing on his tail. You'll have to read *Tom's Tail* by Arlene Dubanevich to find out what happened then, but I bet you can guess. (LP-MP)

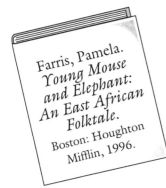

Farris, Pamela. *Young Mouse and Elephant: An East African Folktale*. Boston: Houghton Mifflin, 1996.

When Grandfather Mouse tells Young Mouse that Elephant is the strongest animal on the plains, does Young Mouse believe him? Certainly not!

Young Mouse is very strong and very proud. When Grandfather Mouse warns Young Mouse that Elephant may not want to hear Young Mouse's bragging, Young Mouse sets out to find Elephant. He threatens to "break him apart" and "stomp him to bits."

While Young Mouse seeks Elephant, a big thunderstorm gathers. First Young Mouse encounters Lizard. "Are you Elephant?" "No, I am just a lizard, basking in the sun." Young Mouse stomps his foot on the ground. Just then there is a roaring clap of thunder. Lizard hurries to hide under a bush.

Next Young Mouse meets a zebra, and then a giraffe. Again and again he asks the same question. "Are you Elephant?" Every time he receives "no" for an answer, the sky would darken or the lightning would crash. All by coincidence, you understand.

Finally, Young Mouse does meet the Elephant. And Mouse does threaten to stomp him. Can you guess what happens next? *Young Mouse and Elephant* by Pamela Farris may surprise you. (LP-UP)

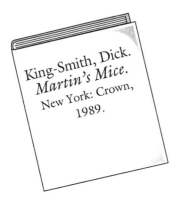

King-Smith, Dick. *Martin's Mice*. New York: Crown, 1989.

Sometimes people keep animals such as mice for pets. Perhaps your class or school has pet mice. *But,* have you ever heard of a cat who keeps mice as pets?

Meet Martin. Martin lives on a farm with his mother, Dulcie Maude, and his sister, Lark, and his brother, Robin. His mother named her kittens after birds.

All but Martin are excellent mousers. Martin goes his own way. He decides that instead of eating mice, he would rather keep them as pets—in an old bathtub up in the loft of the barn. From the moment Martin decides to have mouse pets, his life becomes very complicated.

First, Martin captures a shrewd but pregnant mouse, Drusilla. Soon he is providing for a whole family of mice. Martin's father, Pug, a champion mouser, discovers the tub and the mice. Just imagine what occurs next. Can this story possibly have a happy ending? Check out *Martin's Mice* by Dick King-Smith. (UP)*

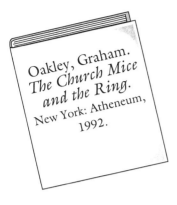

Oakley, Graham. *The Church Mice and the Ring.* New York: Atheneum, 1992.

I t was a nice day, but certainly not an ordinary day, when Percy, a strange puppy, showed up in the churchyard. Humphrey, one of the church mice, listened to Percy's story. He had been a Christmas gift, but things just hadn't worked out. Percy was abandoned. The mice, who knew what it was like not to be wanted, asked Percy to stay around the churchyard.

Then, the very first night, Percy gobbled down all the mice's food. The next morning, the mice determined how they would find a home for this cheese-gobbling puppy.

First, they arranged for Polly, a young girl, to find Percy in the churchyard. Polly took Percy home to meet her parents, but Percy, in a fit of nerves, did everything wrong. Polly's parents asked Percy to leave. Polly's parents were willing for Polly to have a dog. But it had to be a well-behaved dog.

Polly's parents referred to Percy as "that horrid beast." Humphrey the church mouse had his work cut out for him. Somehow, he had to get Polly's parents and Percy together. That was where the ring came into the story.

Humphrey decided that if Percy were a hero and found Polly's mother's ring, certainly Polly would be allowed to keep him. But the ring wasn't lost. When it was lost, Percy wasn't the one to find it. And when the police got involved. . . . I'll say no more. Read *The Church Mice and the Ring* by Graham Oakley to see how the church mice save the day. (MP)

Bibliography

Barklem, Jill. *The Secret Staircase.* New York: Philomel, 1983.

A family of mice live royally in the Old Oak Palace. Every mouse in the forest is busy preparing for the MidWinter Feast. Primrose and Wilfred, mice children, are sent to the attic to practice their poem for the feast. In the attic, they discover a secret staircase and a wonderful surprise. (MP)

Brett, Jan. *Town Mouse, Country Mouse.* New York: G. P. Putnam's Sons, 1994.

Everyone is familiar with the tale of the country mouse and the town mouse, but this story takes the folktale down a different path. Two mice couples exchange homes, and the fun follows. Jan Brett's illustrations create a wonderfully rich setting. (LP-UP)

Burton, Robert. *The Mouse in the Barn.* Milwaukee: Garth Stevens Publishing, 1988.

This nonfiction book covers a broad range of information on mice. It details the types of mice, their habitats, their social life, and why they are viewed as pests. The book contains many photographs, charts, and a glossary. (UP)

Carle, Eric. *Do You Want to Be My Friend?* New York: Thomas Y. Crowell, 1971.

A lonesome little mouse goes from page to page of the book repeating the same question: "Do you want to be my friend?" As he asks animal after animal, the page shows only the tail of the animal. Then the reader turns the page and sees the whole animal. This is a good book for predicting what comes next. (LP)

Cleary, Beverly. *Ralph S. Mouse.* New York: Dell, 1983.

A motorcycle-riding mouse named Ralph S. (for Smart) Mouse lives up to his name. His decision to go live at an elementary school leads to many exciting adventures. (UP)*

Dubanevich, Arlene. *Tom's Tail.* New York: Viking, 1990.

Tom, the cat, was no longer acting like a cat. He was sleeping all the time, and the mice in the house started to live it up. They had a great time until they touched Tom's tail. (LP-MP)

Farris, Pamela. *Young Mouse and Elephant: An East African Folktale*. Boston: Houghton Mifflin, 1996.

A brash mouse declares he is the strongest mouse on the African plains. To prove this he goes in search of Elephant. What happens when he finds Elephant makes this book worth reading. (LP-UP)

Fisher-Nagel, Heiderose and Andreas Fisher-Nagel. *A Look Through the Mouse Hole*. Minneapolis: Carolrhoda Books, 1989.

This book contains photographs of the entire life span of a house mouse. It defines a mouse's enemy and explains how the mouse survives. Other species of mice are described. (MP-UP)

Hoffman, Mary. *The Four-Legged Ghosts*. New York: Dial Books for Young Readers, 1993.

A mouse named Cedric changes the lives of the children in the Brodie household in unimaginable ways. When Alex receives Cedric as a gift, he is pleased and surprised. But when Cedric proves to have magical abilities and begins to bring back the ghosts of every pet that has ever lived in the Brodie household, things get out of control. (MP-UP)*

Holabird, Katherine. *Angelina's Ice Skates*. New York: Clarkson Potter, 1993.

Angelina, the mouse, is skating at the local pond, practicing for the New Year's eve party. Spike and Sammy, two bullies, keep interrupting her skating and spoiling everyone's fun. Mrs. Mouseling comes up with a great idea and solves everyone's problem. This is one of a series of Angelina books. (MP)

Hurd, Thacher. *Little Mouse's Birthday Cake*. New York: HarperCollins, 1992.

It's Little Mouse's birthday, but all his friends are too busy to help him celebrate. Little Mouse decides to go skiing by himself, and then his birthday really starts to go downhill. He finds that this is no way to spend his birthday. (LP-MP)

Ivimey, John. *The Complete Story of Three Blind Mice*. Boston: Joy Street Books, 1990.

Although the mice in this tale do suffer blindness, and their tails are shortened by a carving knife, through twists and turns, the story actually arrives at a happy, humorous ending. (LP-MP)

Iwamura, Kazuo. *Fourteen Fieldmice and the Winter Sledding Day*. Milwaukee: Garth Stevens Children's Books, 1991.

Do you ever wonder what mice do all winter? In this fantasy, the wood mouse family builds sleds, eats jelly rolls, and waits for the blizzard to end and the fun to begin. This is one of the Fourteen Fieldmice series of books. (MP)

King-Smith, Dick. *Martin's Mice*. New York: Crown, 1989.

Martin, one of three siblings, is a gentle-hearted cat. Instead of being a mouser, he is a mouse keeper. That's right, he keeps mice as pets. This is a gentle, humorous story that children of all ages would enjoy. (UP)*

Kraus, Robert. *Another Mouse to Feed*. New York: Windmill/Wanderer Books, 1980.

When a mouse is left on their doorstep, Mr. and Mrs. Mouse must think seriously before taking the mouse into the family. They already have 31 children. How will they manage with 32 children? You'll be surprised. (LP-MP)

Kraus, Robert. *Whose Mouse Are You?* New York: Macmillan, 1970.

Through a series of questions, a little mouse recovers a mother from a cat; a father from a trap; a sister far away, and a brother—wait a minute—is there a brother? (LP)

Lionni, Leo. *Mr. McMouse*. New York: Alfred A. Knopf, 1992.

How did Timothy, the city mouse, become Mr. McMouse and an honorary Field Mouse at that? In this story, Timothy runs from the city, meets up with the field mice, and wins the respect of all. (MP)

Lobel, Arnold. *Mouse Soup*. New York: Harper & Row, 1977.

When Mouse is captured by the weasel and discovers that he is the main ingredient of mouse soup, he saves himself by telling stories—for no soup is good without adding stories. This book is available in Spanish as *Sopa de Raton*. (LP)

Miller, Edna. *Mousekin's Fables*. New York: Prentice-Hall, 1982.

For this book, Aesop's fables have been adapted to fit the Mousekin stories. The forest animals are the characters of the fables. There is a fable for each month of the year, and of course, each fable contains a moral. (MP-UP)

Numeroff, Laura Joffe. *If You Give a Mouse a Cookie*. New York: Harper & Row, 1985.

Talk about consequences! Here we have an entire book of humorous consequences that result from a child giving a mouse a cookie. (LP)

Oakley, Graham. *The Church Mice and the Ring*. New York: Atheneum, 1992.

When Percy, a homeless pup, shows up in the courtyard, the church mice welcome him. When he gobbles down a week's supply of their food, though, the church mice recognize that something must be done. What they do and how they do it makes for a very intriguing story. This book is one of the Church mice series. (MP)

Ostheeren, Ingrid. *Jonathon Mouse, Detective*. New York: North-South Books, 1993.

The farmer's wife is uncharacteristically grouchy. The animals discover the reason for her mood: she has lost her favorite locket. After a meeting of all the farm animals, Jonathan, mouse detective, starts putting the clues together. (MP)

Potter, Beatrice. *The Two Bad Mice Pop-up Book*. New York: F. Warne, 1986.

What awful mischief can two mice, Hunca Munca and Tom Thumb, get into when they go into the nursery dollhouse? Trouble a-plenty! This book tells an amusing tale of mischief and mayhem. (LP-UP)

Schories, Pat. *Mouse Around*. New York: Farrar, Straus & Giroux, 1991.

This wordless book will stimulate storytelling from kindergarten through third grade. The illustrations take the viewer along for the trip as a young mouse leaves his family and goes to town. (LP-UP)

Smith, Wendy. *Twice Mice*. Minneapolis: Carolrhoda Books, 1989.

Thelonius Mouse is really excited when his father tells him there will soon be an addition to the family. That excitement changes with the arrival of two sisters. How will Thelonius respond? (LP)

Steig, William. *Amos and Boris*. New York: Farrar, Straus & Giroux, 1979.

Amos, a mouse, and Boris, a whale, meet when Amos falls from his ship at sea and Boris saves him. Eventually Boris returns Amos to shore. Will Amos ever be able to repay Boris? That is precisely the rest of the story. (MP-UP)

Stevenson, James. *The Stowaway*. New York: Greenwillow Books, 1990.

The story of Hubie and his family going to France on an ocean liner is illustrated cartoon-style. At first, Hubie dislikes the ocean liner, but that changes when he meets Claude, the stowaway. (MP-UP)

Stolz, Mary. *Tales at the Mousehole*. Boston: Godine, 1992.

This is a story of two brother mice, Ozzie and Bob. They are pantry mice and have a friend in the house cat, July. When they decide to leave the house and live elsewhere, lessons are learned by all. (UP)*

Titus, Eve. *Anatole*. New York: McGraw-Hill, 1956.

Anatole was an extraordinary French Mouse who bicycled around Paris each evening collecting food for his family. One evening he overhears the conversation of humans. What he hears changes his life. Be sure to become acquainted with Anatole. There are several other books that feature Anatole the Mouse. (LP-MP)

Van Laan, Nancy. *A Mouse in My House.* New York: Alfred A. Knopf, 1990.

This story is told in rhyme. It starts with a mouse in the house and ends with an entire zoo. (LP)

Wells, Rosemary. *Noisy Nora.* New York: Dial Press, 1973.

Noisy Nora has a reason for making all that noise, but no one, not one person in her family, pays attention to her. Finally, Noisy Nora runs away. This delightful story is told in rhyme. (LP)

Wheeling Across the Curriculum

Art

- For a good fall activity, have the children trace around a mouse pattern. Then collect seeds from grasses or pumpkins, any kind of seeds. Next have the children paste the seeds within the outline of the mouse to make a texture drawing. (LP-MP)

- After reading *Ralph S. Mouse* by Beverly Cleary, have the children design a hiding place for Ralph's new car. (UP)

Language Arts

- Have children retell their favorite mouse story on audiotape. (LP-MP)

- Have the children act out *If You Give a Mouse a Cookie* by Laura Joffe Numeroff. Older children can write a short script. (LP-UP)

- Children can write new lyrics to the song "Three Blind Mice," starting with the line "Three happy mice" or "three tired mice." (MP-UP)

- At the library, ask the children to find a poem about mice. (UP)

- Choose one of the children's favorite authors of mouse stories. Ask the children to dictate or write a letter to that author. Use E-mail if it is available. (LP-UP)

Mathematics

- Give each child a length of string 3–4 inches long. This is the average length of the house mouse's tail. Have the children measure their desks and tables and themselves in mouse tails. (LP-MP)

- Do the same activity as above, but instruct the older children to convert the mouse tail measurements to inches. (UP)

- Cut out circles of different sizes (1″, 1½″, 2″, 2¼″, etc.). Just for fun, tell the children these are mouse ears. Then have them arrange the "mouse ears" from largest to smallest. (LP)

Science

- This activity will take a little preparation. Collect pictures of fish, birds, insects, and mammals. Label four boxes or trays as "fish," "bird," "insect," or "mammal." Pass the pictures out to the children. Talk about what characteristics make a bird different from a mammal, which is different from an insect and different from a fish. Have kindergartners categorize their pictures and place them in the correct trays. (LP)

- Try a similar exercise with older children. Instead of having the children sort the pictures, have the children work in pairs and complete a Venn diagram. (MP-UP)

- If you have access to Internet, get information on the care of mice. (UP)

Mouse Shapes

Mathematics (LP)

Directions: Cut out the shapes. Glue the circle to the triangle at the x. Glue the square to the triangle at the l. Attach a 4-inch string tail at the s. This provides the bookmark.

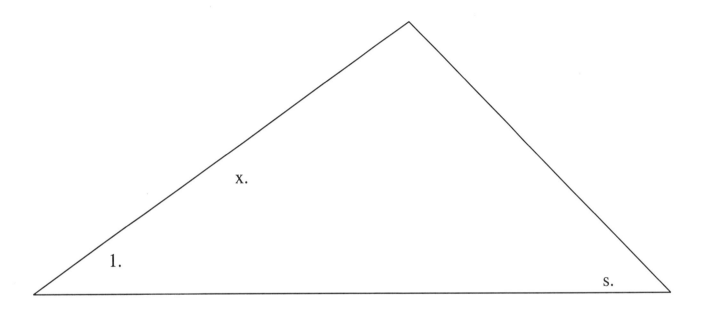

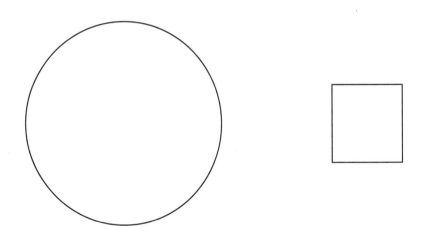

Mouse Hole

Reading (UP)

Directions: Use your very best imagination and draw what you think a mouse's home would look like. Pretend you are looking through a mouse hole.

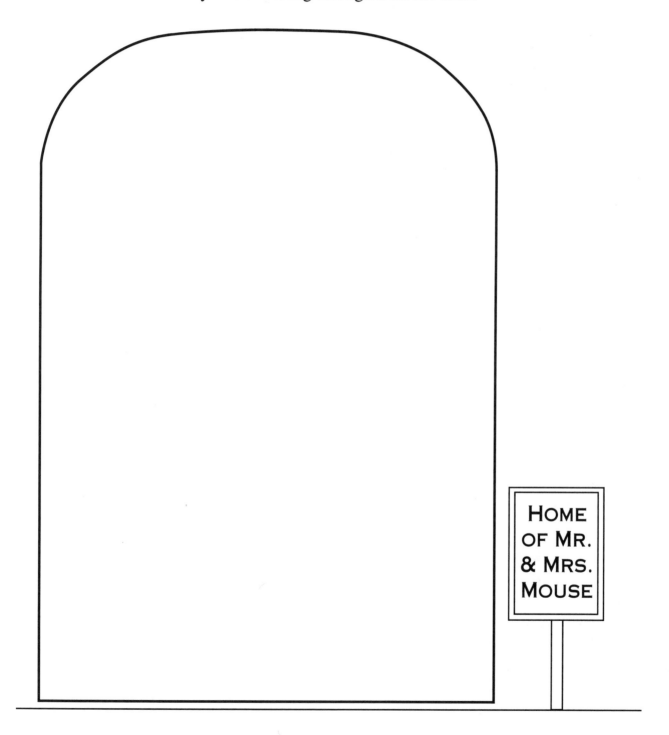

HOME
OF MR.
& MRS.
MOUSE

A Mouse's Day at School

Language Arts (MP-UP)

Directions: Pretend you took your pet mouse to school. Write what happened in the diary entry below.

Today's Date: _____

_____

_____

_____

_____

_____

_____

_____

_____

_____

This diary belongs to

_____

Who can define a monster? Is it a ghost, a werewolf, a dragon, or a witch? Are all monsters bad? What about Mercer Mayer's monster in *There's a Nightmare in My Closet?* It is hardly too terrifying, but for young children monsters can be a source of safe fright. In this chapter, we've included books that identify those feelings that children have about "monsters," whatever form they may take. Most are monsters that will scare deliciously and delightfully. These monsters may be tame compared to what the children have available to them on TV, but we think the children will enjoy these books and, we hope, so will you.

A Rolling Start

Read *The Toll-Bridge Troll* by Patricia Rae Wolff to the children.

- Ask them how they would handle the troll in that same situation.

- Create a bulletin board using the dust jacket from the book, and post the children's replies around it. Label the bulletin board, "How to Deal with a Troll."

- Another fun activity to do after reading this book is to have several riddles written out and placed in a jar. Choose a child to play the troll. Have each child in turn draw a riddle and try to stump the troll. If the troll cannot answer the riddle, the child wins a safe passage over the "bridge." Choose whatever you like to be the bridge—whether it is passage to a section of the library or permission to rejoin the group.

- If the troll answers the riddle correctly, then the child who presented the riddle becomes the troll.

Booktalks

Lindgren, Astrid.
The Ghost of Skinny Jack.
New York: Viking Kestrel, 1988.

Do you believe in ghosts? Do you like to hear ghost stories? Well, the two children in this story love to visit their grandmother and hear the story of Skinny Jack.

Now, Skinny Jack lived a long, long time ago. He was a mischievous fellow. He once tried to scare the church organist to death. But the tables were turned and Skinny Jack ended up scaring himself so badly that his blood turned to ice. The church people didn't know what to do with him, for he was neither dead nor alive. They simply propped him up on the road leading to the church. He stayed there for many a year until a young woman, on a dare, brought him into the house of the parson. She then tried to take him back to his place, but the ghost of Skinny Jack gripped her tightly and forced her to take him to the organist's grave. The organist forgave Skinny Jack, and his body turned to a pile of dust.

Or so it seems. But is the ghost of Skinny Jack really gone? The children in the story must walk home from their grandmother's house. They choose to take a shortcut, and as it is getting dark, something happens that might interest you. If you are curious, you will have to read *The Ghost of Skinny Jack* by Astrid Lindgren to discover the rest of the story. (MP-UP)

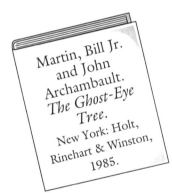

Martin, Bill Jr. and John Archambault.
The Ghost-Eye Tree.
New York: Holt, Rinehart & Winston, 1985.

Have you ever had that shivery, goose bumps feeling down your back on a dark and windy night? Has your mother ever sent you on an errand on a dark and windy night? And have you ever seen a ghost on a dark and windy night?

The ghost-eye tree grows along the path a little boy and his sister must take when they go to get milk from the other side of town. Their mother sends them on this errand on a dark and windy night.

The little girl isn't afraid, but her little brother is feeling nervous. Then they safely pass the oak tree on their way to get milk. They laugh and dance with relief to be safely by the tree.

The way back home turns out to be a different story. If you have ever felt that shivery goose bump feeling down your back on a dark and windy night, then you must read the story of *The Ghost-Eye Tree* by Bill Martin Jr. and John Archambault. (LP-UP).

Pilkey, Dav.
Dragon Gets By: Dragon's Second Tale.
New York: Orchard, 1991.

Would you like to meet a friendly, not-so-bright Dragon? You probably would enjoy this dragon. When he is tired, he gets everything mixed up. Do you ever do that? Well, in the story, Dragon reads the eggs and fries the morning paper. He butters his tea and sips his toast. He keeps getting everything backward. When he opens his closet and it is dark in there, he thinks its nighttime and goes back to bed.

This book has five chapters about this mixed-up dragon. If you enjoy laughing, read Dav Pilkey's *Dragon Gets By.* (MP-UP)*

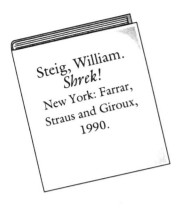

Steig, William.
Shrek!
New York: Farrar,
Straus and Giroux,
1990.

Can you imagine a monster who can spit a flame 99 yards, who smells so bad the flowers wilt when he comes by, and who gives any snake that bites him convulsions? And to boot, he is super-ugly. This monster's name is Shrek.

One day, Shrek leaves the hole where he was born. He sets out to see the world. He comes upon a witch in the forest. She predicts that Shrek will win the hand of a princess—and not only a royal princess, but one who is uglier than Shrek.

As Shrek proceeds, he meets an awful dragon, a talking donkey, and a nutty knight. Shrek overcomes all obstacles, only to give himself a terrible fright in the hall of mirrors. There, all he can see are monsters as ugly as he. When Shrek realizes it is his image in the mirrors, he proceeds to the great hall. There he finds the ugliest of princesses.

Will Shrek find true happiness. Will the princess marry him? Read William Steig's *Shrek!* It's a story you won't soon forget. (UP)

Wolff, Patricia
Rae.
*The Toll-Bridge
Troll.*
New York: Harcourt,
Brace, Jovanovich,
1995.

On the first day of school, Trigg did not wish to be late. He rushed through breakfast, hurriedly hugged his mother, and ran off to school. But on his way to school, Trigg had to cross a bridge, and by this bridge lived a troll. What would you do if you had to go to school by way of a troll bridge? [Pause for the children's responses.]

The first day Trigg was stopped by the troll and asked to pay a penny to cross the bridge. Trigg, being a very clever boy, asked the troll to answer his riddle. If he could answer the riddle, Trigg said he would give the troll the penny. Well, the troll got the riddle wrong. Trigg had free passage across the bridge.

Trigg realized that he had been lucky to outwit the troll. So on the second day, he had an even more difficult riddle. The troll tried very hard to answer the riddle, but once again he was wrong. He was very angry and made terrible troll noises. I wonder what a troll noise sounds like? [Pause for responses.] But back to the story. On the third day, Trigg told the troll that he had no more riddles. He did promise to give the troll six pennies if the troll could answer his question.

To discover what question leads Trigg and the Troll to a solution to their problem, you'll just have to read *The Toll-Bridge Troll* by Patricia Rae Wolff. And don't forget to keep a supply of riddles in your head. They just might come in handy if ever you meet a troll. (LP-UP)

Bibliography

Anderson, Wayne. *Dragon.* New York: Green Tiger Press, 1992.

This is a story, gently told, of a dragon. The dragon is seeking its identity because it does not know what it is. Only when led by a child to a far-off land does the creature learn its true identity. (UP)

Arnold, Tedd. *Five Ugly Monsters.* New York: Scholastic, 1995.

An easy count-to-five book that parodies the rhyme about five little monkeys jumping on the bed. Bright, action-filled illustrations will keep the reader's interest. (LP)

Bright, Robert. *Georgie and the Robbers.* New York: Doubleday, 1963.

Georgie is a friendly ghost who lives in the attic of the Whittakers, an older couple. One night the Whittakers go out, and the robbers arrive. With the help of some animal friends, Georgie manages to "spook" the robbers, and all ends well. (LP)

Eccles, Jane. *Maxwell's Birthday.* New York: Tambourine Books, 1991.

On Maxwell's birthday, he eats Monster Crunch and gets a Walk Monster and licorice snakes. When he opens the gift from Aunt Jane, Maxwell gets what he's always wished for and the rest of his birthday is very scary, indeed! (MP)

Galdone, Joanna. *The Tailypo: A Ghost Story.* New York: Seabury Press, 1977.

A classic scary tale of a creature that returns to claim what is his. An old man cuts the tail off a creature. Not only that, the old man eats the tail. The following night the creature comes back looking for its tail. The suspense rises as the old man becomes fearful, and the creature claims its tail. (MP-UP)

Goode, Diane. *I Hear a Noise.* New York: E. P. Dutton, 1988.

Great illustrations tell the story of a little boy who calls for his mother when he hears a noise outside his window. The noise grows louder, and the boy's calls to his mother are more frantic. The intervention of the mother of the noisy monster brings this story to a happy conclusion. (LP)

Hawkes, Kevin. *Then the Troll Heard the Squeak.* New York: Lothrop, Lee & Shepard, 1991.

This story tells what happens to little girls who jump on their bedsprings at night. The story is told in rhyme. (LP)

Hoban, Russell. *Monsters.* New York: Scholastic, 1989.

A little boy who loves to draw monsters begins to worry his mother and father. When he starts drawing a really huge monster, they decide to take him to the doctor. The doctor has the boy finish this monster drawing, which leads to a surprise ending. (UP)

Howe, James. *There's a Dragon in My Sleeping Bag.* New York: Atheneum, 1991.

Dexter, the dragon, has taken over the sleeping bag, the chair, and the home of Alex At least, that is what his older brother, Simon, would like Alex to think. Finally, Alex catches on, and his solution to the dragon problem is quite creative. (LP-UP)

Hutchins, Pat. *The Very Worst Monster.* New York: Greenwillow, 1985.

Baby Billy Monster is the worst monster in the world, until his sister Hazel figures out how to become the very worst monster. She does this by giving baby Billy away. She then gets all the attention she craved. (MP-UP)

Krauss, Robert. *The Phantom of Creepy Hollow.* New York: Warner Junior Books, 1988.

The mystery of who put bubble-blowing solution in the brass section of the orchestra can only be solved by Mummy Dearest. Mummy not only solves the mystery but also reveals the Phantom of the Opry. (MP-UP)*

Lindgren, Astrid. *The Ghost of Skinny Jack.* New York: Viking Kestrel, 1988.

This classic ghost story is repeated many times by a loving grandmother. She tells her grandchildren about Jack, the most terrible ghost. The children love the story until it is time to walk home. Then the walk through the forest becomes a shivery, scary adventure. (MP-UP)

Martin, Bill Jr. and John Archambault. *The Ghost-Eye Tree.* New York: Holt, Rinehart & Winston, 1985.

In this wonderful tale with great illustrations, two children are sent to the edge of town for a pail of milk. To get to the milk, they have to pass the ghost-eye tree. They also feel the childhood dread of walking by something very frightening and the exuberance of surviving the experience. (LP-UP)

Mayer, Mercer. *There's a Nightmare in My Closet.* New York: Dial Books for Young Readers, 1968.

In this popular book about monsters, a little boy confronts the "nightmare" in his closet, only to discover that this "nightmare" is as frightened of him as he has been of the monster. (LP-MP)

Moncure, Jane Belk. *Magic Monsters Act the Alphabet.* Elgin, Ill.: Child's World, 1980.

The children will have a frighteningly good time going through the alphabet, from apes to zombies, with the magic monsters. (LP)

Mueller, Virginia. *Monster Goes to School.* Morton Grove, Ill.: Whitman, 1991.

When Monster goes to school, he readily answers the teacher when she asks what time it is. Monster not only tells the time; he makes a clock for the class. (LP-MP)

Paraskevas, Betty. *Monster Beach.* New York: Harcourt Brace Jovanovich, 1995.

This is a story of a little boy who is visiting his grandfather at the beach. He is frightened by a sea monster. As the sea monster takes on alarming proportions, it begins to deflate—and turns into a wonderful inflatable toy. (LP)

Parish, Peggy. *No More Monsters for Me!* New York: Harper Trophy, 1981.

When Minneapolis Simpkins's mother says no pets, she means "no pets." However, when Minneapolis finds a little monster, brings it home, and hides it in the basement, she has no idea of the dilemma in which she will find herself. (UP)*

Pilkey, Dav. *Dragon Gets By: Dragon's Second Tale.* New York: Orchard, 1991.

Dragons should be fearsome beasts and strike terror into the hearts of all. This dragon however, is more likely to have you laughing than shaking with terror. Enjoy the story of one mixed-up dragon. (MP-UP)*

Polacco, Patricia. *Babushka Baba Yaga.* New York: Philomel, 1993.

This is a story of a misunderstood monster. Baba Yaga is the last of her kind living in the forest. She longs for the company of a child. When she discovers a babushka and the love of a child, her life changes. The illustrations add greatly to the charm of this story. (LP-MP)

Regan, Dian Curtis. *The Thirteen Hours of Halloween.* Morton Grove, Ill.: Whitman, 1993.

This is a great Halloween take-off on the Twelve Days of Christmas. Instead of a partridge in a pear tree you get a vulture in a dead tree. The illustrations are light-hearted and not in the least bit scary. (LP-UP)

Schwartz, Alvin. *Ghosts: Ghostly Tales from Folklore.* New York: HarperCollins. 1991.

This "I Can Read" book contains seven different ghost stories. The stories vary from one about a bully ghost who ends up in a green bottle to one about a set of teeth found in a graveyard by a little old woman. This collection is sure to please younger children. (MP)

Sendak, Maurice. *Where the Wild Things Are.* New York: Harper & Row, 1963.

The night Max, a mischievous little boy, sails off to where the Wild Things are, is the start of an adventure that has captivated all readers for years. The Wild Things are monsters of strange shapes and sizes who make Max their king. Max does finally return to his bedroom to discover his dinner awaiting him. (LP-MP)

Solotareff, Gregoire. *Never Trust an Ogre.* New York: Greenwillow Books, 1988.

There is one mean ogre who lives alone in the woods. He has eaten his mother, his father, his sisters, and all the animals he could chase and catch. He is now too fat to chase the animals, so he plans to trick them by acting friendly and gaining their trust. (LP-MP)

Steig, William. *Shrek!* New York: Farrar, Straus & Giroux, 1990.

This book is a rather perverse approach to the "fairy tale prince meets princess" line. Shrek is the ugliest monster on earth. As he sets out to see the world, he meets a witch who predicts that he, Shrek, will conquer a knight and win the hand of a princess, who, in fact, is uglier than Shrek. (UP)

Stevenson, James. *Emma.* New York: Greenwillow Books, 1985.

> Emma, a young witch, gets tricked by two truly nasty witches, Lavinia and Dolores. Emma, her friend Botsford, the cat, and Roland, the owl, put their heads together and get the better of Lavinia and Dolores. The story is presented humorously in cartoon format. (MP-UP)

Treece, Henry. *The Magic Wood.* New York: Willa Perlman Books, 1992.

> This poem by Henry Treece describes a young boy's imaginary trip through a forest at night. A forest full of eyes and tiny cries sets the mood for a rather scary adventure. The illustrations suit the mood perfectly. (UP)

Wagner, Jenny. *Amy's Monster.* New York: Viking, 1990.

> Amy is sent to spend her summer vacation with her cousins, Jocasta and Meredith. These twins are very clever and very mean when no one is looking. They play many tricks on Amy, but Amy comes up with a good trick of her own—she finds a monster under her bed. (MP-UP)

Winthrop, Elizabeth. *Maggie and the Monster.* New York: Holiday House, 1987.

> Maggie has a monster in her room. She tells her to leave; she makes a sign saying "STAY OUT"; but not until she asks the monster how she can help it does Maggie solve the puzzle. (LP-MP)

Wolff, Patricia Rae. *The Toll-Bridge Troll.* San Diego: Harcourt, Brace, Jovanovich, 1995.

> A troll tries to prevent a little boy, Trigg, from crossing the bridge to school, only to be outwitted by Trigg and his riddles. Great illustrations. (LP-UP)

Wylie, Joanne and David Wylie. *The Gumdrop Monster.* Chicago: Children's Press, 1984.

> Colorful monsters fill the pages of this book, with each monster representing a particular color. A little boy asks each differently colored monster for gumdrops. In the end, he finds all the colors on the gumdrop monster. (LP)

Wheeling Across the Curriculum

Art

- To make wonderful ghosts, starch pieces of cheesecloth and drape them over balloons. (LP-UP)

- Have the young children make a print by placing a dot or two of tempera paint on the crease of a paper and folding the paper, inkblot style. They can then finish their monsters with bits of torn paper. (MP-UP)

- Have the children make paper plate monster masks. (LP-UP)

Drama

- Ask the children to tell their favorite ghost story. They become the storytellers. (UP)

- Put a few scary props into a paper sack and ask a pair of children to make up a story appropriate for those props. (MP-UP)

Language Arts

- Ask the children to describe settings in which their scary stories will take place. (LP-UP)

- Have the children brainstorm scary word vocabularies. Place these words on an overhead transparency and display them whenever the children write their own stories. Put a little pulled-apart Dacron filler over the words to set the mood. (MP-UP)

- Have the children make-up a monster alphabet by thinking of one scary word for each letter. Illustrate the monster alphabet. (LP)

Mathematics

- Give the children some "monster" math problems. Use standard story problems from a text, but make the characters in the problem "monsters." For example, if Joe sees three ghosts on Monday and Mary sees five ghosts on Thursday and B. J. sees one ghost on Friday, how many ghosts were seen in all? (LP-UP)

- Practice counting with the younger children. Use black beans as bats and white beans as ghosts. (LP)

Reading

- Have the children make lists of Facts and Fables for such "scary" creatures as black cats, bats, and ghosts. (UP)

- Read Mercer Mayer's *There's a Nightmare in My Closet* and have the children illustrate what nightmare is in their closet. (LP-UP)

- After listening to, or reading, several scary stories, have the children make a clay model of their favorite character. (LP-UP)

Monster Math

Mathematics (LP)

Directions: Count each type of creature. Count all the creatures on the page. Write your answers next to the words *Total*.

Total _____

Total _____

Total _____

All Creatures Total _____

A Change of Heart

Reading (UP)

Directions: After reading *Shrek!* by William Steig, write a new ending in which both Shrek and the princess turn into a fairy tale prince and princess.

That's Quotable

Language Arts (MP-UP)

Directions: Think about how you would respond to a monster who demanded your lunch money. Write down three different responses. Use quotation marks.

I said, _____

I said, _____

I said, _____

This chapter will deal with the term *multiculturalism* in its broadest meaning. The books selected reflect the stories, arts, or way of life of a given people. The bits and pieces of various cultures presented in these books will help children have a better understanding of people throughout the world. Our world does become smaller day by day, and our contact with others, through travel or the Internet, makes it imperative that we approach cultures other than our own with an informed mind. The books selected will also help children to understand that children are the same everywhere and have similar feelings, joys, and problems universally.

A Rolling Start

Read *Mama, Do You Love Me?* by Barbara Joosse. This is a good introduction to a multicultural unit.

1. After discussing the book with the children, go back through the book and list all the animals that were presented. Place the names of the animals on 3x5″ cards. Practice reading the words.

2. Do the same thing with articles of clothing.

3. Go back and look at words for shelter and transportation. On a piece of paper, write all the words in a circle around the word *Inuit.* Decorate a bulletin board with the children's pictures of their vocabulary word of choice.

Booktalks

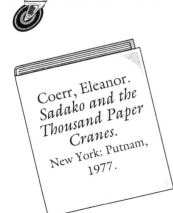

Coerr, Eleanor. *Sadako and the Thousand Paper Cranes.* New York: Putnam, 1977.

Do you like to read stories about children in different countries? Do you like to know how the children react to situations, even very serious ones? In this story of Sadako, a young Japanese girl, you will learn about courage and about a loving family.

Sadako is a schoolgirl who loves to run. She is very excited when she is selected to be in the relay race for her school group. She wins the race. She feels a little dizzy, but doesn't tell anyone because she thinks it will pass. Sadako is too busy thinking about running for her class when she is in junior high.

But then Sadako becomes ill and weak. She has to go to the hospital, and there they discover what her illness is. It is the atomic bomb sickness. Sadako was exposed to radiation when the atomic bomb was dropped during the war. What do the atomic bomb sickness, Sadako, and one thousand paper cranes have to do with one another? To find out, read *Sadako and the Thousand Paper Cranes* by Eleanor Coerr. (UP)*

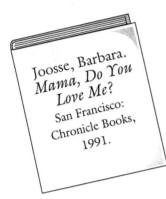

Did you know that the people we often call Eskimos call themselves Inuit? It means "the people." They are the people of the Arctic regions. And do you know what an ermine and a puffin are? You can find out if you read this book. It is about a little girl who innocently asks her mother, "Mama, do you love me?" Can you guess what her mother answers? [Pause for responses.] Then the little girl goes on to ask the question over and over again, each time adding something to the question that will be sure to make her mother say, "No, I do not love you." But the little girl is not successful. Her mother always answers in a truthful, tender, loving way. If you would like to know more about the Inuit people, read *Mama, Do You Love Me?* by Barbara Joosse and be sure to enjoy the illustrations. (LP-UP)

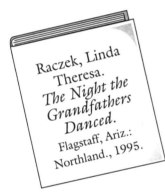

If you have ever wanted to know about Native American dances, you'll have to read about Autumn Eyetoo, a young Ute girl, and her first Bear Dance.

The Utes celebrate the Bear Dance in the spring of each year. This year Autumn Eyetoo is planning to dance. Her day begins with her getting dressed in her special clothes, putting on her beautiful shawl, and wearing a beaded barrette. Autumn then walks to the cleared area where the dance is held. She stops to listen to the musicians. She sees the fry bread stands and finds her friends. Everyone is excited, and the girls know just whom it is they want to dance with.

Soon Autumn goes toward the boy she wants to dance with, but he runs away. At the Bear Dance, the boy must dance if the girl brushes her shawl against him. This is all done in good fun, but still Autumn wonders if she will ever get to dance.

Finally, she has a great idea. She knows how to get to dance, and that is how the story of *The Night the Grandfathers Danced* by Linda Theresa Raczek comes about. You'll just have to read this very unusual book to find out what happens. (UP)

Have you ever moved? Was it from one neighborhood to another, or was it from one part of the country to another? The little boy in this story must move from the East Coast to the Wild West, where Gila monsters really do meet you at the airport.

Let me tell you what else happens when you move to the West. You have to dress up like a cowboy and wear a cowboy hat and spurs. You never get to play baseball because you have to chase buffaloes all the time. And breakfast consists of chili and beans. Have any of you ever eaten chili and beans for breakfast? Do you think it is any better if you happen to live in the West and have to move East?

In the East it snows all the time, and the streets are full of gangsters. There is no space left in the East, and there are alligators in the sewers. Can you believe that? The two boys who meet at the airport believe these facts about the East and the West. Who is right? Which way would you move? To make your decision, read *Gila Monsters Meet You at the Airport* by Marjorie Weinman Sharmat. (LP-UP)

Soto, Gary. *Too Many Tamales.* New York: G. P. Putnam's Sons, 1993.

Have you ever tasted a tamale? Do you know they are part of the Christmas tradition of many Mexican Americans? Every Christmas, families gather to make tamales. It is a very special time. *Too Many Tamales* is the story of Maria, a young girl, who is helping her mother make tamales. While she and her mother are working, her mother takes off her beautiful diamond ring. Maria loves how the ring sparkles. She wishes to wear the ring on her finger, if only for a moment. Maria and her mother make two dozen tamales. Then the whole family arrives to celebrate Christmas. Maria stops making tamales to go to play with her cousins.

Maria and her cousins are having a great time until suddenly she remembers the ring. She runs to the kitchen, but it is gone. There is nothing on the counter but the steaming tamales. Could the ring be inside one of the tamales? How can she find the ring? What would you do? Be sure to devour *Too Many Tamales* by Gary Soto to discover the answer to the puzzle of the missing ring. (MP-UP)

Bibliography

Ancona, George. *Powwow.* San Diego: Harcourt Brace Jovanovich, 1993.

Beautiful photographs capture the fun and excitement of a powwow at the Crow Fair in Montana. Learn about the Fancy, Traditional, Grass, and Jingle-dress dances. The book is a little difficult to read, but the pictures will vividly portray this event for young children. (LP-UP)

Asbjornsen, P. C. and J. E. Moe. *The Man Who Kept House.* New York: Margaret K. McElderry, 1992.

In this humorous Norwegian folktale, a rather grouchy farmer trades places with his wife for one day. He discovers that many things can go wrong. While he is attempting to churn the butter, he gets thirsty and goes downstairs for a beer. While filling his mug, he hears a pig come into the kitchen. That's just the beginning. (MP-UP)

Brown, Marcia. *Once a Mouse.* New York: Charles Scribner's Sons, 1961.

A hermit, in India, is meditating when he sees a tiny mouse run by. He saves the mouse from a crow, but when the mouse is threatened by a large cat, the hermit changes the mouse into a larger cat, then a dog, and finally a tiger. The tiger's pride leads to his humiliation when the hermit changes the very proud tiger into a little mouse once more. (LP-UP)

Bunting, Eve. *Cheyenne Again.* New York: Clarion Books, 1995.

This is a study of the clash of cultures, that of the Cheyenne and white people. It tells of a young Cheyenne boy in the late 1800s who is taken to a boarding school and forced to abandon his own culture. A kind teacher helps the boy maintain his identity, and he becomes Cheyenne again. (UP)

Coerr, Eleanor. *Sadako and the Thousand Paper Cranes.* New York: Putnam, 1977.

The setting is Japan, several years after the explosion of the atomic bomb. Sadako is a young girl now, but she was a baby at the time of the bombing. This story is based on the life and death of a real Japanese girl, who, when she comes down with the atomic bomb disease, decides to fold one thousand cranes for good luck. Sadako dies surrounded by 644 cranes and a loving family. This is a story of beauty and courage. (UP)*

dePaola, Tomie. *Strega Nona: Her Story.* New York: G. P. Putnam's Sons, 1996.

Tomie dePaola has written the history of Strega Nona, from her birth until the day Big Anthony arrived at her door. We now know that Strega Nona learned her magic from her wonderful Italian grandma, Concetta. We also learn that Nona had a friend, Amelia, and we are told about some of the events that shaped Strega Nona's life. We even learn how Strega Nona came to receive the Magic Pasta Pot. (LP-UP)

Ets, Marie Hall. *Gilberto and the Wind.* New York: Puffin Books, 1963.

Gilberto, a little boy, learns about the many moods of the wind. The wind is his playmate when he wants to sail a toy boat or blow soap bubbles. The wind will knock an apple from a tree for Gilberto, but sometimes the wind can be frightening. (LP-MP)

Flack, Marjorie. *The Story About Ping.* New York: Viking, 1933.

Ping was a duck who lived on a Chinese boat on the Yangtze River. Ping lived with his family. Each morning, Ping and his family would go down to the bridge and look for wonderful things to eat. Each night, the master of the boat would call the ducks back to the boat, and the last duck in line would get a spank on the back. One night Ping was the last duck in line. Ping did not want to be spanked, so he hid in the grasses and did not return to the boat. Thus began Ping's adventure. (LP-MP)

Fox, Mem. *Koala Lou.* San Diego: Harcourt Brace Jovanovich, 1988.

Mem Fox writes about a baby koala bear, Koala Lou. Koala Lou's mother loves her baby dearly. Koala Lou decides to enter the Bush Olympics. She trains and trains, always sure that her mother loves her dearly. When the Olympics come and Koala Lou doesn't win, will her mother still love her? This is a terrific book to use to introduce the animals of Australia. (LP-MP)

Friedman, Ira R. *How My Parents Learned to Eat.* Boston: Houghton Mifflin, 1984.

A little girl tells the story of how her parents met one another in Yokohama, Japan. Her father is an American sailor and her mother a Japanese schoolgirl. Each has to overcome the fear of eating in the style of the other's culture. The chopsticks seem formidable to the sailor, as do the knife and fork to the Japanese schoolgirl. In overcoming their fears about that one small cultural difference, they overcome many cultural differences. This is a really delightful story. (UP)

Havill, Juanita. *Jamaica Tag-Along.* Boston: Houghton Mifflin, 1989.

Jamaica follows her older brother, Ossie, to the park and wants to play basketball with his friends. Of course, he doesn't want his tag-along sister playing, even if she is pretty good. Jamaica then wanders to the sandlot, where she turns her back on Berto, a toddler, when he tries to help her build a castle. Jamaica then realizes that she's just done what her brother did to her. Jamaica and Berto make a great sandcastle, and when Ossie's game is over, she even lets him help. (LP-UP)

Joosse, Barbara. *Mama, Do You Love Me?* San Francisco: Chronicle Books, 1991.

A young Inuit girl asks her mother repeatedly, "Mama, do you love me?" The mother responds to the child in charming and loving ways. The illustrations provide a look at the Inuit culture and environment. A picture glossary is included. (LP-UP)

Keats, Ezra Jack. *Hi, Cat.* New York: Macmillan, 1970.

> Archie and Peter live in the city. One day Archie is walking down the street eating an ice cream cone. He passes a cat and says, "Hi, Cat." That simple greeting starts a chain of interactions between the boys, the cat, and Willie, the dog. The illustrations depict the neighborhood of the inner city perfectly and add to the charm of the story. (LP-UP)

Lester, Julius. *John Henry.* New York: Dial Books for Young Readers, 1994.

> This book is a richly illustrated tale of John Henry, an African American folk hero. John Henry is special from the day he is born. He is big and he is strong. He has many adventures, but is remembered best for the race to dig a railroad tunnel through a mountain. He goes up against a steam drill. John Henry puts all his strength into this task and wins, but at the cost of his life. (MP-UP)

Mathis, Sharon Bell. *The Hundred Penny Box.* New York: Viking, 1975.

> This is the story of an African American family: Michael, his great-great-aunt Dew, and Michael's parents. Aunt Dew is one hundred years old and has a box that holds one hundred pennies, one for each year of her life. She also has a story for each penny. She tells Michael the stories as he counts the pennies. Michael's mother wants to throw the box away, and in that conflict lies a very human story. (UP)

McDermott, Gerald. *Raven: A Trickster Tale from the Pacific Northwest.* San Diego: Harcourt Brace Jovanovich, 1993.

> When Raven comes to the world, all is in darkness and the men and women are cold. Raven, through his powers of trickery, changes himself into a pine needle. The daughter of the Sky Chief drinks the water with the pine needle in it, and the folktale of how Raven brought light to the people begins. (MP-UP)

Parish, Peggy. *Ootah's Lucky Day.* New York: Harper & Row, 1970.

> Ootah is an Eskimo boy who wants very much to go hunting with the men. His father tells him he is too young to hunt, so Ootah sets off to hunt by himself. He harpoons a walrus and then has to puzzle out how to get the walrus back to his village. All works out well. This is an I Can Read book. (LP-MP)

Polacco, Patricia. *Just Plain Fancy.* New York: Bantam Books, 1990.

> Naomi and Ruth, two Amish girls, find a very different-looking egg while collecting eggs outside the henhouse. They keep the egg, and when it hatches, they name the chick Fancy. But soon it is apparent that this is not a chick like all the rest. The girls try to hide Fancy, so that it would not be shunned by the Amish folks for not being plain. During a barn building, Fancy makes its escape and displays its plumage for all the world to see. It is a peacock. (LP-UP)

Provensen, Alice and Martin Provensen. *Shaker Lane.* New York: Viking Kestrel, 1987.

> *Shaker Lane* begins with the Herkimer sisters having to sell a part of their land to make ends meet. Slowly, a neighborhood of very interesting people forms a community. All goes along quite well until there is a water project, and Shaker Lane ends up under water. The people from Shaker Lane leave, and what remains of the area is now called Reservoir Road. This is an interesting study of the changes in neighborhoods. (UP)

Raczek, Linda Theresa. *The Night the Grandfathers Danced.* Flagstaff, Ariz.: Northland, 1995.

> The illustrations tell the story of Autumn Eyetoo and her first Bear Dance. Autumn has her shawl, her new clothes, and her beaded barrette. She even has her eye on a young man, but much to her dismay, he runs away as she tries to brush her shawl against him. This story of the Ute Bear Dance and a young girl's solution to finding a dancing partner will delight the reader and reveal something of the Ute culture. (UP)

Sharmat, Marjorie Weinman. *Gila Monsters Meet You at the Airport.* New York: Macmillan, 1980.

> An East meets West story, in which two boys exchange their stereotypical views of each other's planned destinations. Do Gila monsters really meet you at the airport in the West? Only if there are two days of spring and summer back East. This is a humorous account of regional differences. (LP-UP)

Soto, Gary. *Too Many Tamales*. New York: G. P. Putnam's Sons, 1993.

When the family gathers at Christmas, Maria helps her mother prepare tamales. Maria notices her mother's diamond ring on the counter and decides to slip it onto her thumb. She soon forgets about the ring, and when she does remember, it is no longer on her thumb, and the tamales are steaming on the platter. The illustrations capture the mood of the story perfectly. (MP-UP)

Wheeling Across the Curriculum

Art

- Have the children design a totem pole. (LP-UP)
- Demonstrate how to weave a simple design. Use paper or yarn. (LP-UP)
- Teach the children how to make a coiled pot with clay. (LP-UP)
- Invite a basket maker to demonstrate her or his craft. (LP-UP)

Drama

- Using puppets or a flannel board, ask the children to act out the story *Mama, Do You Love Me?* by Barbara Joosse. (LP-UP)
- After reading *Jamaica Tag-Along* by Juanita Havill, ask for volunteers who would like to act out how they respond when a younger sibling tags along. (UP)

Language Arts

- Ask the children to make a list of traits or things we do that tell others we are Americans. (UP)
- Teach the children five greetings in other languages. (LP-UP)
- Teach the children how to say "thank you" in five foreign languages. (LP-UP)
- Have the children draw pictures to illustrate the contrast between city and country cultures. (LP-UP)
- Ask the children for the names of people from various countries, for example, Japan/Japanese, Guatemala/Guatemalan, France/French, Philippines/Filipino, Mexico/Mexicans, Nigeria/Nigerians. (UP)

Library Skills

- Show the children how to use a children's atlas to find a map of the country they have been reading about. (MP-UP)

Mathematics

- Have the children make a human graph of the various cultures within the classroom. To create a human graph, have the children physically move to designated spots and line up to form a graph. (LP-UP)
- Teach the children the numbers from one to 10 in another language. (LP-UP)

Music

- Listen to music from around the world. (LP-UP)
- Display pictures of instruments from various cultures. (LP-UP)

Reading

- Have the children read various versions of the Cinderella story. (UP)
- Have the children read folktales from various countries. Keep track of which countries the children chose by sticking pins in a world map. (MP-UP)
- Have the children retell their favorite folktale. (LP-MP)

Social Studies

- Have the children bring in a family recipe. Identify the cultural origin, if possible. Make a book of these recipes. (LP-UP)
- If any of the children's parents or grandparents or the children themselves are from a different country, invite them to share their experiences of living in another country and compare them to living here. (LP-UP)
- When the children read a book about another country, have the children write a review of the book within the outline of the country. For instance, if a child read *Strega Nona* by Tomie dePaola, he or she would draw an outline of Italy and then write the review inside the outline. (UP)
- Plan a cultural "trip" with the children, and select a book for each culture "visited." End the trip with a cultural project. The children can either draw what they learned or produce something from one of the various cultures visited. (UP)

Learning from Others

Reading (LP-UP)

Directions: Choose a country and find that country in a primary atlas. Write the name of the country at the top of the paper. In each of the squares below, draw one thing you learned about another culture. It can be food, housing, holidays, or anything you have learned.

Country_____

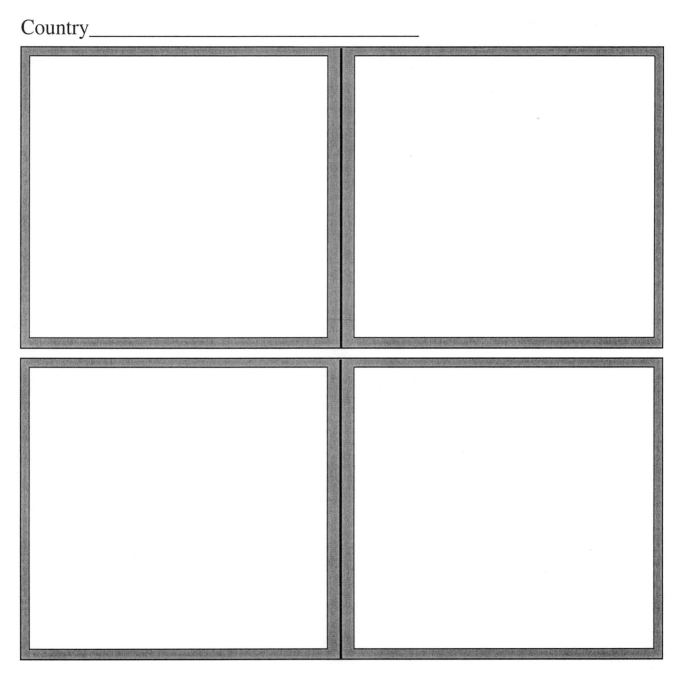

Our Classroom Culture

Social Studies (UP)

Directions: Work with a partner. After the word *Definition,* write down your definition of culture. Using that definition, what do you think you can say about the classroom culture? What actions and habits do you have in your classroom?

Definition:

_____

_____

_____

_____

_____

Our classroom culture:

_____

_____

_____

_____

_____

Dressing Right

Social Studies (MP-UP)

Directions: People in different lands sometimes dress differently than we dress. Draw clothes on the doll that show the traditional costume for a country of your choice.

CHAPTER 11

...⊹⊹BOOK, LINE, AND SINKER: OCEAN WORLD

It can be as peaceful as a lullaby. It can be as ferocious as a man-eating shark. It blankets three-fourths of our world. It is home to such varied creatures as sea horses, eels, puff fish, and blue whales. We dive beneath it, float on top of it, and play beside it. The ocean has many moods and seasons.

The books featured in this chapter run the gamut from photo essays to fantasy. Each selection provides information about the ocean. The readers will be certain to fall under the lure of the ocean and surface with a new appreciation for it.

A Rolling Start

1. Choose the Reading Rainbow video *Dive to the Coral Reefs*, which features *Dive to the Coral Reefs* by Elizabeth Tayntor. Show the segment that features the book of that title. Mute the sound and have the children concentrate on the colors and shapes that they are viewing. Pause the video and have the children describe what they've seen.

2. When the children have finished watching the video, give them an 8″ round piece of blue construction paper. Ask the children to draw one thing they would like to see if they dove to the coral reefs. Colored chalk works well with this drawing exercise.

3. Display these drawings by hanging a series of three circles vertically from the ceiling.

Booktalks

Cooper, Susan. *The Selkie Girl.* New York: Margaret K. McElderry, 1986.

Do you like tales of mystery and magic? If you do, you'll be interested in the old Scottish tale of the Selkie girl.

This is a story about Donallen, a young man who lived by himself next to the sea. His parents were dead, and he had not married. He had a dog to herd sheep and a cat to catch mice, but often he was lonely.

One day Donallen was gathering seaweed by the shore when he was surprised to see three beautiful girls at the edge of the water. He was immediately enchanted with the fair-haired girl. He knew this was the girl he would marry.

Donallen's dog growled when it saw the girls. To Donallen's amazement, the girls grabbed a shapeless ball of fur and jumped into the sea. They instantly became Selkies, or gray seals.

Donallen met an old man and told him he had fallen in love. The old man told Donallen how he could catch the Selkie girl, on the very same date the following year on the seventh day of spring at high tide. The old man also gave Donallen a warning: "A wild creature will always go back to the wild in the end."

Do you think Donallen will be able to capture the Selkie girl? Will this story have a happy ending? If you like mystery and magic, remember to read *The Selkie Girl* by Susan Cooper. (UP)

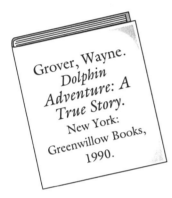

Grover, Wayne. *Dolphin Adventure: A True Story*. New York: Greenwillow Books, 1990.

Have you ever thought about going underwater like a scuba diver? What would you look for underwater?

Wayne Grover went scuba diving off the coast of Florida. This was one of his favorite things to do. One day when he was diving away from the other divers, he had quite an exciting experience.

As he was swimming along, he heard a clicking sound. The clicking sound became louder and louder, and a family of dolphins appeared. A mother, father, and baby dolphin were right there in front of Wayne. The baby dolphin had become tangled in a fishing line and had a hook imbedded close to its fin.

The dolphins swam around and clicked as though asking for help. Wayne finally decided to reach out and touch the baby. The baby was frightened and dashed away to its mother. The baby dolphin was then wedged between its mother and father and brought back to Wayne. This was a clear signal that the parents wanted Wayne to help the baby.

Wayne took out his knife and cut away the fishing line. Then he noticed that the hook was so deeply imbedded that it too would have to be cut out. Will the dolphins permit him to do this? Will the blood in the water draw sharks? To find out what happens to Wayne and the dolphin family, be sure to read *Dolphin Adventure* by Wayne Grover. (UP)

Samton, Sheila White. *Jenny's Journey*. New York: Viking, 1991.

If you had a friend who moved far away and was lonely, what would you do?

Jenny's friend, Maria, has moved far away and is very lonely. Jenny writes to tell Maria she misses her also. She draws a picture for Maria. It is a picture of a little boat that Jenny will sail in to visit Maria. Then Jenny imagines what it would really be like to cross the sea; she imagines how alone and lonely she would be on her boat. But Jenny decides she wouldn't be lonely for long. The sea creatures would be with her, and there are ocean liners that would sail by her. Jenny has an entire fantasy planned out. She even thinks about bad things happening at sea, such as a storm with waves as high as mountains. Jenny keeps on writing as she pictures the whole voyage to see Maria. Finally she imagines she sees land., Who is there to greet her? Now it is your turn to imagine, or perhaps you'd rather just read the book *Jenny's Journey* by Sheila White Samton. (LP-MP)

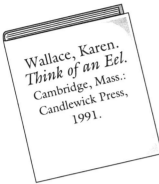

Wallace, Karen.
Think of an Eel.
Cambridge, Mass.:
Candlewick Press,
1991.

Did you know that some eels migrate? Can you describe an eel? This book describes eels as something that swims like a fish and slides like a snake.

There is a place off the coast of Bermuda (an island in the Caribbean) called the Sargasso Sea. In that sea, eel eggs hatch and become eels. A baby eel looks like a leaf. It is born in the spring, and it will travel to either North America or Europe. There are hundreds of these tiny leaflike eels swimming on top of the waves. Up in the sky are hungry seagulls, who pluck the eels out of the water and eat them.

The eels that make it to Europe arrive around Christmas. It is too cold to keep swimming on their journey to the rivers, so they wait offshore and become elvers. They stop looking like leaves and start looking more like adult eels.

When spring arrives, the elvers swim up the rivers and slip into slimy mudholes. They'll stay there for three years, growing into mature adult eels. Silver eels then wait for a moonless night to start their journey back home. Sometimes there are so many eels waiting to go back to the ocean that they get tangled up in a big ball. Would you like to see an eel ball? [Pause for the children's responses.]

To find out about the eels' lives and what happens when they finally get home to the Sargasso Sea, read *Think of an Eel* by Karen Wallace. (UP)

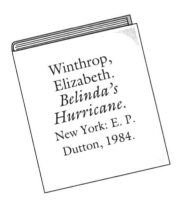

Winthrop,
Elizabeth.
*Belinda's
Hurricane.*
New York: E. P.
Dutton, 1984.

How would you feel if you knew a hurricane was headed your way? Would you want to leave and hurry to safe ground, or would you want to stay and see it for yourself? [Pause for the children's responses.]

Belinda, the little girl in this story, felt both scared and excited when she found out that a hurricane was headed toward the island. She had spent the entire summer with her Grandma on an island. Now it was the end of summer and time for her to go home. Belinda had worked hard all summer trying to earn $15.00 for a shell necklace to give her grandmother. When she went to buy the necklace, she discovered it had been sold. Belinda didn't know what to do. She had had her heart set on that particular necklace.

However, with the hurricane coming, Belinda soon had other things on her mind. No one could leave the island. Mr. Fletcher, Grandma's neighbor, and his dog, Fishface, came to the house to ride out the hurricane. First, the rain started to hit against the house. Then the wind groaned and moaned as it squeezed the house. Mr. Fletcher and Fishface stayed by themselves in the dining room. Suddenly, Mr. Fletcher ran from the dining room, followed by Fishface. Mr. Fletcher ran out into the storm to get his tools from his house. Belinda had always been afraid of Fishface. But when Mr. Fletcher returns to the house without Fishface, and when the water starts coming under the door of the house, this story takes an unexpected turn. What do Belinda, Grandma, and Mr. Fletcher do? Where is Fishface? And what will become of the shell necklace that Belinda wants to buy? To discover how it all comes together, you'll just have to take a deep breath and read *Belinda's Hurricane* by Elizabeth Winthrop. (MP-UP)

Bibliography

Burton, Jane. *Coral Reef.* New York: Dorling Kindersley, 1992.

This book has a ton of facts about the animals and plants of the coral reef. The photographs are spectacular. This book has a glossary and index. Each section has a small "guess what" paragraph, which is sure to hook the reader. (UP)

Calhoun, Mary. *Henry, the Sailor.* New York: Morrow Junior Books, 1994.

Henry, the cat, is a stowaway when the Man and the Kid go sailing. Henry enjoys being at sea, until the Man falls overboard and Henry has to help the Kid save him. The Man tells Henry he is one great stowaway. (MP-UP)

Chermayeff, Ivan. *Fishy Facts.* San Diego: Gulliver Press, 1994.

This brilliantly illustrated book presents fish facts on every page. There is much to learn about fish, from flounder to cowfish, in this book. (LP)

Cole, Joanna. *The Magic School Bus on the Ocean Floor.* New York: Scholastic, 1992.

One of the series of Magic School Bus trips, this one goes to the ocean floor. Ms. Frizzle, the teacher, explains what the children are seeing in her own Ms. Frizzle way. This book is full of information on subjects ranging from tidal pools to mammals in the sea to rivers in the oceans. This book provides a very enjoyable fact-filled trip. (UP)

Conrad, Pam. *The Lost Sailor.* New York: HarperCollins, 1992.

This is the story of a lucky man who happens to be a sailor. He always sails his ship in the right direction and is never lost. He sails into terrible storms, and his ship, the Promise, always comes through the storms unscathed. Then one day he sails into such a tremendous storm—a storm that leaves the sailor shipwrecked on an island, but still "a lucky man." (MP-UP)

Cooper, Susan. *The Selkie Girl.* New York: Margaret K. McElderry, 1986.

The myths and legends of the sea are part of the folklore of Scotland, and one of the Scots' favorite stories is about the Selkie girl, a beautiful young woman who transforms herself into a gray seal. This particular tale recounts how Donallen, a young Scot, captures a Selkie girl for himself. (UP)

Ehlert, Louis. *Fish Eyes: A Book You Can Count On.* New York: Harcourt Brace Jovanovich, 1990.

Not only can the children count their way through this book while enjoying the brightly colored fish, but they can learn how to add by one on each page. Just follow the guide fish. (LP)

Ganeri, Anita. *I Wonder Why the Sea Is Salty and Other Questions About Oceans.* New York: Kingfisher, 1995.

In 31 pages of fascinating questions and short answers, this book resolves a variety of questions children have about the oceans of the world. There is an index. (UP)

Garland, Sherry. *The Summer Sands.* San Diego: Harcourt Brace, 1995.

This is a picture book study of sand dunes as viewed by a brother and sister visiting their Grandpa. They visit in both the summer and winter, and they observe both the destruction and rebirth of the sand dunes. (UP)

Gibbons, Gail. *Sharks.* New York: Holiday House, 1992.

This book provides many facts about sharks in easy-to-understand language. The illustrations enhance the factual information. The children will have a basic idea about types of sharks and their habits after they read this book. (MP-UP)

Grover, Wayne. *Dolphin Adventure: A True Story*. New York: Greenwillow Books, 1990.
    In this fascinating story of an encounter between a diver and a family of dolphins, a baby dolphin has become entangled in fishing lines. The adult dolphins appear to recruit the diver for assistance. (UP)

Hoff, Syd. *The Lighthouse Children*. New York: HarperCollins, 1994.
    Sam and Rose live by a lighthouse at the edge of the sea. When a terrible storm damages the lighthouse, Sam and Rose are forced to move inland far from the sea and their "lighthouse children," the seagulls. But the story ends happily, when the seagulls find Sam and Rose. (LP-MP)

Hulme, Joy N. *Sea Squares*. New York: Hyperion Books for Children, 1991.
    This is a counting book with a twist, or should I say, square. The book depicts the creatures of the deep while counting their eyes, fins, and tails. Then it goes one step further: each page provides the square of the number it is depicting. (LP-UP)

Limmer, Milly Jane. *Where Will You Swim Tonight?* Morton Grove, Ill.: Albert Whitman, 1991.
    This counting book combines fantasy and fact. A little girl pretends she is a fish and chooses various marine creatures with which to swim. (LP-UP)

Lionni, Leo. *Swimmy*. New York: Pantheon Books, 1963.
    This is a delightful story of how one fish can make a difference. That one fish is Swimmy. When little fish scatter in fear of the big fish, Swimmy comes up with a wonderful idea. He has all the small fish swim together in the shape of one large fish. The fish learn a lesson in cooperation. (LP-UP)

Mahy, Margaret. *The Great-White Man Eating Shark: A Cautionary Tale*. New York: Dial Books for Young Readers, 1990.
    What a nasty child is Norvin! He pretends to be a shark so as to have the beach to himself. He does get his comeuppance when a real white shark takes a romantic interest in him. (LP-UP)

McPhail, David. *Pigs Ahoy!* New York: Dutton Children's Books, 1995.
    Once again the pigs of *Pigs Aplenty, Pigs Galore* are up to their freewheeling fun. They make mischief below deck, on deck, and especially in the dining room. Can this be why they end up adrift in an overloaded lifeboat? (MP-UP)

Nakawatari, Hautaki. *The Sea and I*. New York: Farrar, Straus & Giroux, 1992.
    Follow a young boy as he spends his day waiting for his father to return to his island from the sea. Hautaki paints a beautiful portrait of the sea and its shoreline. (LP-UP)

Pallotta, Jerry. *The Underwater Alphabet Book*. Watertown, Mass.: Charlesbridge Publishing, 1991.
    Go through the alphabet learning about tropical fish, coral reefs, and other interesting marine facts. The illustrations are realistic and very colorful. (LP-UP)

Paraskevas, Betty. *On the Edge of the Sea*. New York: Dial Books for Young Readers, 1992.
    In this fantasy tale, a little boy dreams he lives in a sand castle. A perfect day at the beach ends when someone says, "Get up, sleepyhead." (MP-UP)

Pfister, Marcus. *The Rainbow Fish*. New York: North-South Books, 1992.
    Rainbow fish learns the lesson of sharing from the wise octopus. At first Rainbow fish was proud of his shiny scales and would not share them, but loneliness teaches him a lesson about how to make new friends. (UP)

Rand, Gloria. *Aloha, Salty*. New York: Henry Holt, 1996.
    Salty, the dog, and Zack are sailing from Alaska to Hawaii. Salty has been with Zack at sea many times, and the voyage is routine until a big storm hits. Both Zack and Salty are knocked overboard and washed up onshore. (MP-UP)

Rockwell, Ann and Harlow Rockwell. *At the Beach*. New York: Macmillan, 1987.
    A little girl and her mother go to the beach. With straightforward, colorful illustrations, this picture book tells us the details of that morning. (LP)

Rotner, Sherry and Ken Kreisler. *Ocean Day.* New York: Macmillan, 1993.

This is a photographic essay of a day at the ocean. A little girl, Emily, discovers sand patterns, tide pools, seashells, and beach grass, plus the fun of playing in the sand and water. (LP-UP)

Ryder, Joanne. *A House by the Sea.* New York: Morrow Junior Books, 1994.

A small boy imagines what it would be like to have a house by the sea. He imagines seals, crabs, whales, and finally a little girl for a playmate. (MP-UP)

Samton, Sheila White. *Jenny's Journey.* New York: Viking, 1991.

When Jenny's good friend moves away, Jenny takes a fantasy voyage across the sea to visit her. Jenny imagines a boat and a trip across the ocean. This imaginary journey includes sea creatures and even a storm at sea. (LP-MP)

Sis, Peter. *An Ocean World.* New York: Greenwillow Books, 1992.

In an almost wordless book, a whale leaves Ocean World and enters the vast ocean. The whale encounters many ocean creatures but does not meet another whale until the very, and we suspect happy, end. (LP-UP)

Wallace, Karen. *Think of an Eel.* Cambridge, Mass.: Candlewick Press, 1991.

The story of the eels that hatch off the coast of Bermuda and swim to Europe to develop into adult eels. This true nature story is stranger than fiction. (UP)

Winthrop, Elizabeth. *Belinda's Hurricane.* New York: E. P. Dutton, 1984.

A little girl visiting her grandmother for the summer is disappointed when she saves her money to buy her grandmother a shell necklace, only to discover that the necklace is not there when she goes to buy it. Then a hurricane hits the island and prevents her from leaving, but provides Belinda with an exciting adventure. (MP-UP)

Wheeling Across the Curriculum

Art

- Have the children cut fishy shapes from tissue paper, then layer the shapes between blue tissue to give a water effect. (UP)

- Ask the children to design a sand castle. (LP-UP)

- If sand is available, make sand sculptures. (LP-UP)

- Have the children draw a miniature aquarium on construction paper and fill it with thumbprint fish. (MP-UP)

Language Arts

- Have the children write a letter, to be placed in a bottle and sent to sea. It should follow the friendly letter format. (UP)

- Have the children work cooperatively to make a dictionary of "ocean" words. (UP)

- While reading *Think of an Eel* by Karen Wallace, have the children listen for five descriptive words and five action words. (LP-UP)

Mathematics

- After reading *Swimmy* by Leo Lionni, draw the shape of a large fish. Show the children the shape of a small fish and have them estimate how many small fish would fit into the large fish shape. (LP-UP)

- Using marine motifs, make up several patterns. For example, five whales, two seashells, and three sea horses. Have the children predict what shape and number come next. (LP-UP)

- Have the children make up patterns and share them with one another. (LP-UP)

Reading

- Decorate a chair as Neptune's throne. Children may share books they've read while sitting in that chair. (MP-UP)

- Bring in travel magazines and let the children cut out pictures about beaches, paste them into books, and write or tell stories about them. (LP)

- Play an environmental tape of ocean sounds as you read an ocean story. *Ocean Day* by Sherry Rotner and Ken Kreisler would work well with a tape. (LP-UP)

Social Studies

- Use a globe and locate all the oceans. (LP-UP)

- Use a map and find the beach closest to your location. (LP-UP)

- Look for articles on pollution of the oceans in periodicals. (UP)

- Have the children write why we should keep the oceans clean. (MP-UP)

Science

- Have the children gather information about the water cycle and draw a diagram of it. (UP)

- Conduct experiments about evaporation. Fill jars with the same amount of water and set them in different places around the room. Place one under a light and one in the dark. One should have a plastic cover, and one should not have a lid. Have the children draw conclusions about evaporation rates. (LP-UP)

- Try adding two or three teaspoons of salt to the water and see if that effects the evaporation rate. (LP-UP)

- Have the children use pictures from magazines to classify marine life into three categories: mammal, plant, or fish. (MP-UP)

My Aquarium

Art (LP-UP)

Directions: Draw whatever you would like to have in your aquarium. It can be as big or as little as you want to make it.

Fish Facts

Science (MP-UP)

Directions: Write down five facts you have learned about fish.

1. _____

   _____

2. _____

   _____

3. _____

   _____

4. _____

   _____

5. _____

   _____

What a Catch

Reading (LP-UP)

Directions: Design a book jacket for your favorite book about the ocean.

..✖ WRINKLED, WISE, AND WONDERFUL: OLD PEOPLE

CHAPTER 12

Older people play an important part in children's lives. The books selected for this chapter show older people in a variety of ways: as grandparents, as successful older people, and as older people who become part of the family through "adoption." As children read these stories, they will remember the older people in their lives as well as realize the contributions older people make in all our lives.

A Rolling Start

1. To introduce older people to children, have an older person from the community come in and talk about his or her life and what has happened in the community over the years.

2. Have children make a wall of words that describe or are associated with people who are older, such as *wrinkled*, *Grandma*, *Grandpa*, *Nana*, and so on.

3. Children can bring in pictures (photographs) of an older person who is important to them. They can attach the picture to a paragraph about what this person means to them. These can be made into a bulletin board display.

Booktalks

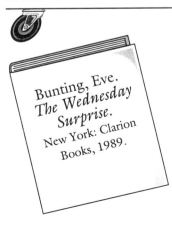

Bunting, Eve. *The Wednesday Surprise.* New York: Clarion Books, 1989.

Wednesday is a special night for Anna. Her Grandma rides the bus across town to take care of her while her mother works late and her brother Sam is at basketball practice. Each week when Grandma is due to arrive, Anna watches out the window for her to come. When she sees her Grandma, she runs down the stairs to meet her. Grandma carries a heavy, lumpy bag full of books each week. When dinner is over and the dishes are done, Anna and Grandma take out the books. They read book after book. They are working on a surprise for Anna's father when he comes home for his birthday celebration. He drives a big truck and comes home on the weekends. Saturday comes and they get ready for the party. Grandma comes with her big bag of books. After father has opened his presents, Anna gives the bag of books to her Grandma. What is the surprise? Who will read the books? To find out what the surprise is, read *The Wednesday Surprise* by Eve Bunting. (MP-UP)

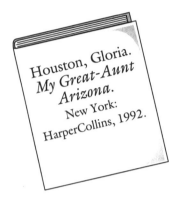

Houston, Gloria. *My Great-Aunt Arizona.* New York: HarperCollins, 1992.

When Arizona was born, a letter arrived for her mother from her Uncle. The letter said that if the baby is a girl, name her Arizona because it is such beautiful country. That is how she received her name, even though she grew up in the Ozarks of North Carolina.

Arizona grew tall, and when she got older she loved to read. She read about faraway places she someday wanted to visit.

However, Arizona never did visit those places. Instead she went over the mountain to go to school. Then Arizona went to school to learn to be a teacher.

At last, she went home to teach where she was raised, to Henson Creek. She taught in the one-room school that was so noisy it was called a blab school. Arizona told the children about the faraway places she had read about.

Eventually Arizona married the carpenter who was building the new school. Arizona became Mrs. Hughes and taught for many more years. She taught until she was old and had white hair.

Did Arizona ever visit the faraway places she read and dreamed about? To find out, read *My Great-Aunt Arizona* by Gloria Houston. (UP)

Miles, Miska. *Annie and the Old One.* Boston: Little, Brown, 1971.

The sun rises and sets; the sheep go out to graze in the morning and come back each night. There is order in Annie's world. Her mother is trying to teach Annie how to weave the rug she is making. Annie would rather be outside with her Grandmother, herding the sheep so that she doesn't work on the rug very much.

Her Grandmother knows that order changes. One day, she tells her family that when Annie's mother finishes the rug, she will return to Mother Earth.

Annie doesn't want this to happen. She decides, if she can keep the rug from being finished, she can keep her Grandmother alive. But each day as her mother works on the rug, it gets bigger. Will her plan work? What will the Old One do if the rug is not completed? To find out what happens to Annie's plan and what the Old One will do, read *Annie and the Old One* by Miska Miles. (MP-UP)

Polacco, Patricia. *Mrs. Katz and Tush.* New York: Bantam, 1992.

What special holidays with special traditions do you celebrate in your family? Larnel meets his neighbor, Mrs. Katz, who lives all alone. Because Larnel doesn't want her to be alone, he takes her a kitten.

Most people think the kitten is ugly because it was the smallest of the litter and has no tail. But Mrs. Katz names the cat Tush and thinks she is wonderful. Larnel gets to know Mrs. Katz because every day, he stops by to play with Tush. Time passes, and it draws closer to the Jewish celebration of Passover. Mrs. Katz teaches Larnel what it means to the Jewish people. Larnel realizes that Mrs. Katz doesn't have anyone to celebrate with, so he asks her if he can celebrate with her. Of course, Mrs. Katz says yes and begins to teach him about the Seder, which is the special feast they will eat.

Over the years, as Larnel grows up, Mrs. Katz becomes his special *bubee,* or grandmother. To find out more about what happens to Mrs. Katz, Tush, and Larnel, about how they celebrate the Seder, and about how their special friendship develops, read *Mrs. Katz and Tush* by Patricia Polacco. (LP-UP)

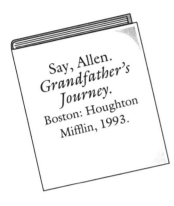

Say, Allen. *Grandfather's Journey.* Boston: Houghton Mifflin, 1993.

Were any of you born in a different country? How about your parents or grandparents? Many people are born in another country and then move to America, where they make a new life. It is not always easy to leave another country, and many people wish to go back to visit or live there again.

The grandfather in this story was born in Japan, where he lived until he was a young man. He came to America on a ship and was amazed at how big the ocean was. In America, he saw many wondrous things that he liked. After a time he returned to his village in Japan to marry his childhood sweetheart. After they were married, he brought her to the new land. They had a home by San Francisco Bay, because of all the places he saw in his travels around America, he loved it best. Soon he had a daughter, and as she grew, he again thought of his faraway home and his childhood in Japan. He decided to move back to his homeland. The years went by, and he had a grandson. The grandson tells the story of what he remembers of his grandfather and the journeys they took. To learn more about these journeys, read *Grandfather's Journey* by Allen Say. (MP-UP)

Bibliography

Ackerman, Karen. *Song and Dance Man.* New York: Alfred A. Knopf. 1988.

Grandpa was a song-and-dance man in the good old days of vaudeville. When the grandchildren come to visit he takes them up to the attic, where the show begins. What kind of dancing and singing will Grandpa do? (LP-UP)

Albert, Richard E. *Alejandro's Gift.* San Francisco: Chronicle Books, 1994.

Alejandro lives alone in the desert. He has his mule for company and a garden to keep him busy. When animals of the desert come to visit the water hole, Alejandro realizes he has been lonely. Alejandro decides to give the animals a gift. This book also has an illustrated glossary about the animals found in the deserts of the Southwest. (UP)

Barrett, Judi. *Cloudy with a Chance of Meatballs.* New York: Atheneum, 1981.

Grandpa is a great storyteller, especially when Henry and his sister are getting ready for bed. He tells them about the town of Chewandswallow. The food for the town comes from the weather. There is orange juice rain and hail like peas. (MP-UP)

Belton, Sandra. *May'naise Sandwiches and Sunshine Tea.* New York: Four Winds Press, 1994.

Big Mama is Little Miss's grandmother. One day, as they are looking at a photo album, Big Mama tells Little Miss about a time when she was growing up and served may'naise sandwiches and sunshine tea to her friend. Little Miss listens to the story and can't wait for the day she can serve such things to her friend. (LP-UP)

Bunting, Eve. *The Wall*. New York: Clarion Books. 1990.

This is a story about a boy and his father who go to the Vietnam Memorial (The Wall) to look for his Grandfather's name. While there, they see many other people looking for names on the wall. The boy also sees the flags and other memorabilia that people have left to remember those whose name are on the wall. (UP)

Bunting, Eve. *The Wednesday Surprise*. New York: Clarion Books, 1989.

Wednesday is a special night for Anna. It is the night her Grandma comes to take care of her. They have a big surprise they work on every Wednesday, to be shared on Anna's father's birthday. (MP-UP)

dePaola, Tomie. *Nana Upstairs, Nana Downstairs*. New York: Putnam, 1973.

Tommy has a grandmother and a great-grandmother. He calls one "Nana Downstairs" because she cooks on the big stove downstairs. His great-grandmother is 94 and must stay in bed. He calls her "Nana Upstairs." (LP-UP)

dePaola, Tomie. *Now One Foot, Now the Other*. New York: Putnam, 1981.

Bobby was named after his best friend, his grandfather Bob. "Bob" was the first word Bobby could say, and Bob taught him to walk. Then his grandfather had a stroke. He couldn't walk or talk. Bobby must help him. (LP-UP)

Flournoy, Valerie. *The Patchwork Quilt*. New York: Dial Books for Young Readers, 1985.

Grandma starts making a quilt from the scraps of the family's shirts and dresses. When Grandma gets sick, what will happen to the quilt? Valerie looks at the quilt and thinks she can finish it! (MP-UP)

Flournoy, Valerie. *Tanya's Reunion*. New York: Dial Books for Young Readers, 1995.

This sequel to *The Patchwork Quilt* starts with Tanya and her grandmother going to the farm where Grandma grew up to get ready for a family reunion. The farm is different than what Tanya expects. She learns about the family history and the family farm. (MP-UP)

Franklin, Kristine L. *The Old, Old Man and the Very Little Boy*. New York: Atheneum, 1992.

Once there was an old man who lived in an African village. The people of the village called him "Old Father" and asked him many questions. Then one day, Old Father tells a very little boy the answer to the question, "Were you ever a little boy?" (LP-UP)

Houston, Gloria. *My Great-Aunt Arizona*. New York: HarperCollins, 1992.

Arizona was born in a log cabin. As she grew up, she dreamed of faraway places that she would one day visit. She never visited those places, but as a teacher she taught her students to love those faraway places. (UP)

Lasky, Kathryn. *My Island Grandma*. New York: Morrow Junior Books, 1993.

Abby spends the summer on an island with her grandmother. They have lots of adventures on the island. Abby learns about the sea, the birds, and the island. (LP-UP)

Martin, Bill Jr. and John Archambault. *Knots on a Counting Rope*. New York: Henry Holt, 1987.

Told in rhyme, this is a Native American story. The boy asks his grandfather to tell him stories about where they came from, about the old ones, and about when the little boy was born. What do the knots mean? How is time measured? (UP)

Miles, Miska. *Annie and the Old One*. Boston: Little Brown, 1971.

Annie lives on the Navajo Reservation. Her mother tries teaching her to weave a rug, but Annie would rather be outside with her grandmother. One day, her grandmother (the Old One) tells her family that when the new rug is completed, she will go to see Mother Earth. (MP-UP)

Munsch, Robert. *Love You Forever*. Ontario, Canada: Firefly Books, 1986.

A new baby is born, and his mother tells him she will love him forever. As he grows, she tells him that she will love him forever. Finally, he is a man and has his own home, but his mother is old and sick. Will he be able to tell her that he loves her forever? (MP-UP)

Nodar, Carmen Santiago. *Abuelita's Paradise.* Morton Grove, Ill.: Whitman, 1992.

Marita's father put her grandmother's, or Abuelita's, rocking chair in her room. She sat in the chair remembering all the things Abuelita had told her about Puerto Rico, or Paradise as she called it. Will thinking about these stories help Marita remember her grandmother after she dies? (LP-UP)

Orr, Katherine. *My Grandpa and the Sea.* Minneapolis: Carolrhoda Books, 1990.

Lila's grandfather is a fisherman who lives on the island of St. Lucia. He is very wise and teaches her many things about life, including lessons about the heart. (MP-UP)

Passen, Lisa. *Grammy and Sammy.* New York: Holt, 1990.

Grammy has come to live forever with Sammy's family. But Grammy and Sammy the cat don't get along. Sammy gets into Grammy's things and tears them up. Then Grammy chases him. Sammy and Grammy need to learn to get along. (LP-MP)

Polacco, Patricia. *Mrs. Katz and Tush.* New York: Bantam Books, 1992.

Larnel goes with his mother to visit a neighbor, Mrs. Katz. He realizes that she is lonely, so he brings her a cat she names Tush. Larnel starts visiting Mrs. Katz and Tush after school, and they become friends. Soon Mrs. Katz is teaching Larnel many things, and their friendship lasts for many years. (LP-UP)

Polacco, Patricia. *Thunder Cake.* New York: Philomel, 1990.

As a little girl, Patricia was afraid of thunder, especially when she was at her grandmother's farm. As the thunder got closer, she would hide under the bed. Then grandma shared with her how to make a thunder cake. (LP-UP)

Say, Allen. *Grandfather's Journey.* Boston: Houghton Mifflin, 1993.

Grandfather was raised in Japan but leaves as a young man to see the world. He has many adventures and settles in California. When his family grows, he takes them back to Japan to live. Then the next generation leaves Japan to see the world. (MP-UP)

Stevenson, James. *We Can't Sleep.* New York: Greenwillow Books, 1982.

When Mary Ann and Louie can't sleep, Grandfather tells them a story of when he was young and couldn't sleep. His story is a wild adventure in which he meets many different animals. What will Grandpa do so that Mary Ann and Louie will sleep? (LP-UP)

Strangis, Joel. *Grandfather's Rock: An Italian Folktale.* Boston: Houghton Mifflin, 1993.

When Grandfather gets too sick to be taken care of at home, his family takes him to a home for old people. His four grandchildren decide they don't want him to leave. They try to think of ways to convince their father to keep the grandfather they love at home. (LP-UP)

Wilder, Laura Ingalls. *Dance at Grandpa's* [adapted]. New York: HarperCollins, 1994.

Adapted from the *Little House* books, this is a story about visiting Grandpa in the big woods. While there, there was a party, and everyone danced. (UP-MP)

Wheeling Across the Curriculum

Art

- Invite older people to share crafts with children, especially if there are local or regional crafts children might not be familiar with. (LP-UP)
- Have children collect old buttons and make button pictures. (LP-UP)
- Children can be taught to knit or crochet by an older person. (MP-UP)

Art/Social Studies

- After reading *Annie and the Old One* by Miska Miles, have children do a paper weaving project. (LP-UP)

- Children can make a diorama of a one-room school in a shoebox after reading *My Great-Aunt Arizona* by Gloria Houston. (UP)

Language Arts

- Children can be instructed to write a letter to residents of a retirement center or nursing home. (LP-UP)

- After writing stories or poems, children can go to a nursing home or retirement center and read them to the residents. (LP-UP)

- Sponsor a Grandparent's Day. Have children write invitations to be given to older people in the community. (MP-UP)

- Children can develop questions to ask an older person in an interview about their life. Arrange for children to complete the interview. (MP-UP)

Language Arts/Social Studies

- After interviewing an older person, children can make a time line showing events in the person's life. The events can be both personal and historical. (UP)

Mathematics

- Collect recipes from children that they have received from a grandparent or other relatives. Have children make some of the recipes, using the measurements for math practice. (MP-UP)

- Direct children to make up math problems using people's ages or the year they were born. (UP)

Science

- After reading *My Island Grandma* by Kathryn Lasky, children can make a moss garden or learn about how birds are born. (MP-UP)

- Children can do research on foods that people need to eat to stay healthy and live a long life. (MP-UP)

- Children can read stories about Navajo rug weaving to determine what plants and seeds can be used to make natural dye for the wool yarn. (UP)

Social Studies

- Tape a "community elder" talking about the "good old days" so that children can listen and learn about life at that time. (LP-UP)

- Ask children to brainstorm ideas for ways they can help or be of service to an older person. (LP-UP)

- Children can interview an older person to find out what life was like without everyday things such as TVs, VCRs, malls, or fast food places. (MP-UP)

- Map skills can be practiced by having children determine on a map where their grandparents or other relatives came from. (MP-UP)

Social Studies/Math

- A survey of older people can be done by children to determine what types of occupations were common 30 to 50 years ago. The results can be put on a graph so children have a visual reference. (MP-UP)

Happy Letter

Language Arts (LP-UP)

Directions: Use this letter form to write a letter to an older person. Have an adult help you mail it.

Wrinkled, Wise, and Wonderful

Reading (LP-UP)

Directions: On the quilt square, write the titles and authors of the books you have read from this chapter.

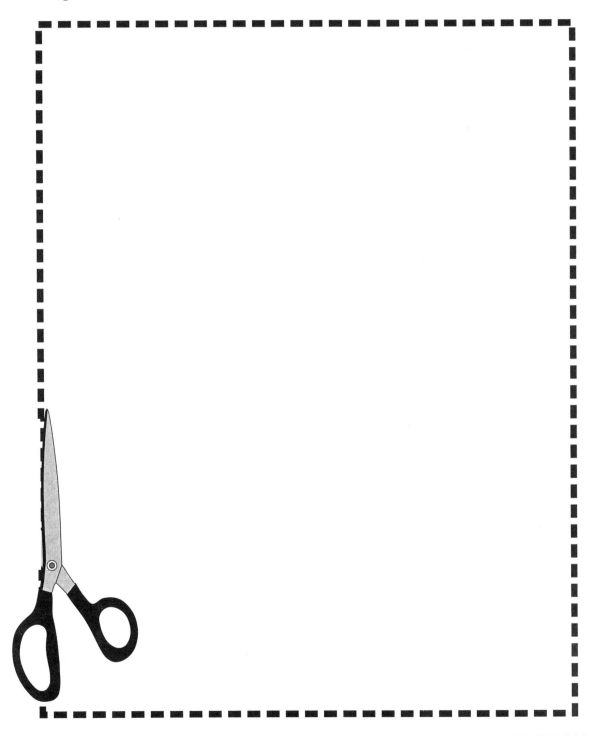

Family Tree

Social Studies (LP-MP)

Directions: Figure out who is your great-aunt. Write your mother's family names on left-hand branches and your father's family on right-hand branches of the tree. Do you have a Great-Aunt Arizona?

From *Books on Wheels.* © 1998 Janice McArthur and Barbara E. McGuire. Libraries Unlimited. (800) 237-6124.

Poetry is something with which children usually haven't had much experience. Also, many children feel that it isn't poetry if it doesn't rhyme. Children often believe nursery rhymes are the only type of poetry.

Most of the books in this bibliography are anthologies or collections of poems. Some books contain poems by the same author and the same subject, and other books are collections by various poets.

Through the activities in this chapter, children can experience poetry that makes them laugh, paints a picture with words, talks about colors, or is just plain fun to listen to.

A Rolling Start

1. Choose one of the color poems from *Hailstones and Halibut Bones* by Mary O'Neill. Ask the children to close their eyes while it is read to them. Afterwards, ask them to relate what they thought as the poem was read to them.

2. Pick a children's poet such as Jack Prelutsky. Select a variety of his poems to be read to the children so they can experience the many different kinds of poetry. After reading several poems, have children make a chart comparing the characteristics of the poems. For example, children may say that one poem made them laugh, and another one used nonsense words.

3. Have children draw pictures of what they visualized as a poem was read to them. Create a bulletin board from their pictures.

Booktalks

de Regniers, Beatrice Schenk, ed. *Sing a Song of Popcorn.* New York: Scholastic, 1988.

This book is a collection of 128 poems selected from poets whose work has been popular for many years. Included are some longtime standards.

The book is divided into nine sections : "Fun with Rhymes," "Mostly Weather," "Spooky Poems," "Story Poems," "Mostly Animals," "Mostly People," "Mostly Nonsense," "Seeing, Feeling, Thinking," and "In a Few Words." Each section contains delightful poems, and the illustrations for each section are done by Caldecott-winning illustrators. These bright illustrations make the poems in *Sing a Song of Popcorn* come alive for the reader.

This collection of poems and illustrations has something for every poetry reader. (LP-UP)

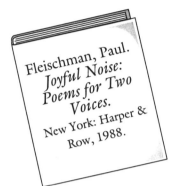

Fleischmann, Paul. *Joyful Noise: Poems for Two Voices.* New York: Harper & Row, 1988.

The poems in this books are written for two people to read. Sometimes the voices read lines together; sometimes they read separately. This format adds to the readers' enjoyment of the poetry.

Each of the poems is about nature. They include poems about grasshoppers and fireflies. In the poem about water striders, the bugs tell about how easy it is to walk on water.

Joyful Noise gives the reader a new slant on poetry and how it can be written as well as read. The poems can also be used in science units on insects. (MP-UP)

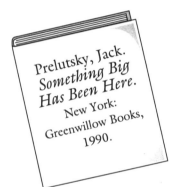

Prelutsky, Jack. *Something Big Has Been Here.* New York: Greenwillow Books, 1990.

This collection of poems by Jack Prelutsky is filled with the humor that has made his poems a favorite among many readers. The title poem, "Something Big Has Been Here," is about big footprints that are found in the snow. What made the footprints? The reader can imagine what the creature looked like.

Other poems, such as "An Elephant Is Hard to Hide," are fun poems in which the reader's imagination can soar. The poems are designed to give children an enjoyable experience with poetry.

If you are looking for a book filled with poems that can be enjoyed by readers of all ages, Jack Prelutsky's book *Something Big Has Been Here* is a good choice. (LP-UP)

Rogasky, Barbara, ed. *Winter Poems.* New York: Scholastic, 1994.

Barbara Rogasky selected 25 poems that are written about the many aspects of winter. There is a poem about the coming of winter with the migration of geese and another poem that was published in Japan about A.D. 905.

The colorful illustrations for all the poems were done by Trina Schart Hyman and enhance the beauty of the poems. To add to the enjoyment of the illustrations, the reader learns from the notes at the beginning of the book that Ms. Hyman has included her family, the house she lives in, herself, and the editor in the illustrations for *Winter Poems*. (LP-UP)

Silverstein, Shel. *Falling Up.* New York: HarperCollins, 1996.

In Shel Silverstein's new book, the reader meets fun new characters. Some of the characters are Screamin' Millie, a girl named Allison with 25 eels, and Headphone Harold. Then there is Reachin' Richard, who doesn't ask for things to be passed but just reaches. What if there was a day just for noise, when girls and boys could make as much noise as they wished?

These are just a sample of the many characters found in *Falling Up*. Adding to the fun of this book are the traditional line drawings of Shel Silverstein. (MP-UP)

Bibliography

Carle, Eric. *Dragons, Dragons*. New York: Philomel, 1991. (Compiler: Laura Whipple.)

This is a compilation of poems about dragons and other monsters. Eric Carle's wonderful illustrations add much to the enjoyment of the poems. (LP-UP)

Charlip, Remy. *Fortunately*. New York: Aladdin, 1993.

This book illustrates a type of poetry children enjoy writing, in which there is cause and effect: Fortunately/Unfortunately or Good News/Bad News poems. This is a simple type of poetry for children to write. (MP-UP)

Chief Seattle. *Brother Eagle, Sister Sky: A Message from Chief Seattle*. New York: Dial Books for Young Readers, 1991.

A narrative poem based on the words of Chief Seattle as his people were sent northward to different lands. He talks about how the eagle is the brother of all people. This poem will inspire all who read it. (LP-UP)

Cohn, Amy, comp. *From Sea to Shining Sea*. New York: Scholastic, 1993.

This collection of poems and songs about America includes many of the traditional poems. Also included are the words and music of many songs that tell of America's history. (MP-UP)

Dakos, Kalli. *If You're Not Here, Please Raise Your Hand: Poems About School*. New York: Four Winds Press, 1990.

This book takes a lighthearted look at school through poems. The book title is also one of the humorous poems in the collection. (LP-UP)

de Regniers, Beatrice Schenk, ed. *Sing a Song of Popcorn*. New York: Scholastic, 1988.

In this compilation of poems on all different topics, each section is illustrated by a Caldecott-winning illustrator, adding much to the poems selected in the book. (LP-UP)

Dragonwagon, Crescent. *Alligators and Others All Year Long: A Book of Months*. New York: Macmillan, 1993.

Each poem in this book is about a month. The illustrations use alligators and other creatures to tell the reader about the months. The book provides a good way for children to study the months of the year. (LP-MP)

Fleischman, Paul. *Joyful Noise: Poems for Two Voices*. New York: Harper & Row, 1988.

The poems are designed for two people to read. The printing on the pages is in columns so that it is easy for the readers to know which part of the poem is theirs to read. A different type of poetry book for children. (MP-UP)

Hopkins, Lee Bennett, ed. *More Surprises*. New York: Harper & Row, 1987.

This is a fun, easy-to-read book of poems for all ages. It contains many poems that can be read aloud by adults to children so they can enjoy poetry. (LP-UP)

Hopkins, Lee Bennett, ed. *Surprises*. New York: Harper & Row, 1984.

The first book edited by Lee Bennett Hopkins contains poems that are about a variety of subjects and are easy to read. These poems help children get a feel for different types of poetry. (LP-UP)

Hudson, Wade, ed. *Pass It On: African-American Poetry for Children*. New York: Scholastic, 1993.

A collection of poems specifically about African Americans, this book is written to give the reader insights into this rich part of American history and culture. (MP-UP)

Lansky, Bruce. *Poetry Party!* New York: Simon & Schuster, 1996.

Do you laugh so hard when you read poetry? This book is designed to make the reader laugh and laugh and laugh. Divided into sections about school, family, and other categories, it is truly a funny book. (LP-UP)

O'Neill, Mary. *Hailstones and Halibut Bones*. Garden City, N.Y.: Doubleday, 1961.

What images do you see when you think of the words *white* or *red* or *blue sky*? This book expresses in poetic form all the images and thoughts that we have in relation to color. It is an excellent book for teaching children about colors. (LP-UP)

Prelutsky, Jack. *The Dragons Are Singing Tonight*. New York: Greenwillow Books, 1993.

This is a collection of poems about dragons. It includes fun poems that all can relate to, such as "A Dragon Is in My Computer." (LP-UP)

Prelutsky, Jack. Holiday Poetry collections.

Each of these short collections written by Jack Prelutsky is about a specific holiday. They are filled with humor and will bring smiles to the readers as well as holiday memories. (LP-UP)

- *It's Christmas*. New York: Greenwillow Books, 1981.

- *It's Halloween*. New York: Greenwillow Books, 1977.

- *It's Thanksgiving*. New York: Greenwillow Books, 1982.

- *It's Valentine's Day*. New York: Greenwillow Books, 1983.

Prelutsky, Jack. *The New Kid on the Block*. New York: Greenwillow Books, 1984.

The title poem of this Jack Prelutsky collection talks about the age-old problem of being new to a place regardless of where it is, home or school. Children will enjoy reading this collection and having it read to them. (LP-UP)

Prelutsky, Jack. *The Random House Book of Poetry*. New York: Random House, 1983.

Jack Prelutsky is the editor of this anthology, and Arnold Lobel is the illustrator. Containing a wide variety of poetry, this book has something for everyone's taste in poetry. (LP-UP)

Prelutsky, Jack. *Something Big Has Been Here*. New York: Greenwillow Books, 1990.

The title poem of this book makes the reader think about what could have left such a big footprint. The poems in the collection are fun poems that all readers will find entertaining. (LP-UP)

Rogasky, Barbara, ed. *Winter Poems*. New York: Scholastic, 1994.

This is a collection of poems that shows the seasons leading up to winter and winter turning into spring. Some of the poems are written by well-known authors such as Shakespeare and Edgar Allan Poe. (LP-UP)

Silverstein, Shel. *Falling Up*. New York: HarperCollins, 1996.

In this book, you meet the same type of characters found in Shel Silverstein's other books. The delightful drawings and poems make this newest book a soon-to-be-favorite of all who read it. (MP-UP)

Silverstein, Shel. *Light in the Attic*. New York: Harper & Row, 1981.

This is the second of Shel Silverstein's books of poetry that children find so enjoyable. This book contains the humorous poems and line drawings he is so well known for. (LP-UP)

Silverstein, Shel. *Where the Sidewalk Ends*. New York: Harper & Row, 1974.

Children have fallen in love with Shel Silverstein's collections of poems. His first book begins his tradition of illustrating the poems with humorous line drawings. (LP-UP)

Stevenson, Robert Louis. *A Child's Garden of Verses*. New York: Scribner, 1905.

This book is considered a classic in the area of children's poetry. Many of the poems, such as "The Land of Nod," have become immortalized. Delightful illustrations add to the books. (LP-UP)

Wheeling Across the Curriculum

Art

- After being introduced to shape poems, children can develop their own shape poem using words such as mountain, ice cream cone, or clouds. (LP-UP)

- Children can make their own dragon and then write a poem about it. (LP-UP)

Art/Language Arts

- After reading *Hailstones and Halibut Bones* by Mary O'Neill, children can pick a color, write a poem about it, and illustrate the poem with that color. (LP-UP)

Art/Listening

- Children can listen to a poem. Afterwards, they can do a finger-painting activity to illustrate the poem they heard. (LP-MP)

Drama/Art

- Divide children into groups. Give each group the name of a poet. They must select several poems by that poet to be presented to the rest of the class in a reader's theater, either acted out or illustrated. (MP-UP)

Health/Drama

- Children can dramatize the poem "Don't You Remember How Sick You Are?" by Kalli Dakos. This poem can also lead to a discussion about health habits. (LP-UP)

Language Arts

- At the beginning of the poetry unit, children can begin copying poems they listen to or they read to make their own poetry anthology. The collection can be bound into a book. (LP-UP)

- After reading "If You're Not Here, Please Raise Your Hand" by Kalli Dakos, children can make a list of the silly parts of the poem. Discussion can take place about what makes poems humorous or funny. (LP-UP)

- Children can write their own poems designed to be read by more than one person. (MP-UP)

- After looking at different poetry forms such as acrostic, cinquain, or haiku, children can write their own poems using one of these poetic forms. (LP-UP)

- Younger children can begin writing "wish" poems. Given the beginning "I wish . . . ," children must finish it. (LP)

- Children can write about their perceptions of school, after reading "A Day in School" by G. Brian Karas. (LP-UP)

- After reading the book *Fortunately* by Remy Charlip children can write Fortunately/Unfortunately or Good News/Bad News poems. (MP-UP)

Language Arts/Art

- After reading the poem "Something Big Has Been Here" by Jack Prelutsky, children can make a list of what they think was there and what it looked like. They can also work in pairs or groups to create a "Big Thing" from the list generated. (LP-UP)

Language Arts/Listening

- As children listen to a variety of poems, have them write the images or thoughts the poetry evokes. After each poem, children can share what they wrote. (MP-UP)

Mathematics

- Children can learn number rhymes such as "One, two, buckle my shoe." (LP-MP)

Mathematics/Art

- Children can make their own number rhyme book by creating their own rhymes and then illustrating them. (LP-UP)

Music

- The lyrics of songs are often poems. Poems can be read to the children so they can find the rhyming words in the lyrics. The poetic elements of the lyrics can also be discussed. (LP-UP)

Science

- "Fireflies," a poem from *Joyful Noise* by Paul Fleischman, can be used to introduce a unit on insects/fireflies. (MP-UP)

- Children can pick a word related to nature and write a haiku poem using that word. The poems can be illustrated and put together in a book. (LP-UP)

Social Studies

- To tie poetry and Social Studies together, children can do research and find poems about other countries or in other languages. (MP-UP)

Good News/Bad News

Creative Writing (LP-UP)

Here is an example of a Good News/Bad News poem:
Good News: Today is my birthday. Bad News: The dog ate my birthday cake.
Directions: In the spaces below write your own Good News/Bad News poems.

1. Good News:

    Bad News:

2. Good News:

    Bad News:

3. Good News:

    Bad News:

What Do You Say?

Language Arts (LP-UP)

Poetry uses lots of different words to express feelings.

Directions: In the bubble by each of the three mouths, make a list of words you can use to express the different feelings portrayed by each mouth.

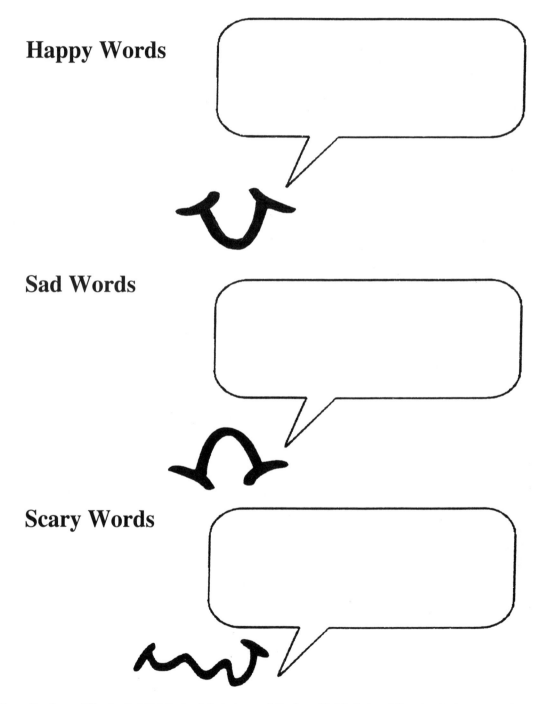

Happy Words

Sad Words

Scary Words

Haiku

Language Arts (MP-UP)

Haiku poetry is about nature and is 17 syllables long. There are five syllables in the first line, seven in the second, and five in the third.

Directions: Use one of the figures above to write about nature in a haiku poem.

Line 1 (5 syllables): _____

_____

_____

_____

_____

Line 2 (7 syllables): _____

_____

_____

_____

_____

Line 3 (5 syllables): _____

_____

_____

_____

_____

When approaching a topic as broad as the planet earth, it is difficult to choose just what approach to take. There is a very eclectic view of the earth presented in the books listed for this chapter. The earth is seen as reason for celebration in some of the books and reason for concern in others. Books on the ecology of ponds, rain forests, and deserts have been included, as well as stories about animals and recycling. The view is broad, but the purpose is to create a sense of wonder and appreciation for the earth.

A Rolling Start

1.   Choose the Reading Rainbow video *The Great Kapok Tree,* which features the book by Lynne Cherry, and show it to the children. The book featured in this video is about a woodcutter in the rain forest who is about to cut down a great kapok tree.

2.   After viewing the video, ask the children to write out what they would whisper into the ear of the sleeping woodcutter, just as the animals in the story whispered into the woodcutter's ear. Post the book cover for *The Great Kapok Tree* on a bulletin board and display the children's responses around the tree. (If the book jacket isn't available, use a map of any country that has rain forests.)

Booktalks

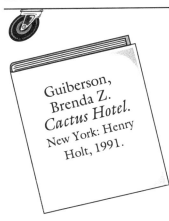

Guiberson, Brenda Z. *Cactus Hotel.* New York: Henry Holt, 1991.

Do you know what a saguaro cactus is? Do you know that they live to be two hundred years old and that it can take a saguaro cactus 10 years to grow only 4 inches? The saguaro cactus is the giant of the Sonoran Desert. They live only in the southwestern United States and northern Mexico. This book tells about the entire life of a saguaro. It starts with the seed that is carried by a pack rat in his whiskers. The rat doesn't even know he's helping the saguaro. Eventually the seed drops out in a good place to grow, and when the rains come, it does start to grow.

What happens to the saguaro as it grows and develops is the rest of this story. It is a hotel to many fascinating creatures, such as the Gila woodpecker, the elf owl, and bats. When one animal moves out of the saguaro, another moves in. Even when the saguaro dies and decays, it provides shelter for ground snakes and insects. You can learn a lot about the desert and saguaro cacti by reading *Cactus Hotel* by Brenda Z. Guiberson. (UP)

Do you know what tadpoles and turtles eat? Do you want to know? If they live in a pond, the tadpoles eat pond ooze. That sounds appetizing, doesn't it? And the turtle, given the opportunity, will eat the tadpole. The nymph dragonfly eats tadpoles also. The nymph lives underwater for a year while it develops, and then one day it crawls out of the pond and turns into a real dragonfly. Fascinating! This book has pictures and explanations of pond life—things that you would never guess happen in a simple lily pad pond. Now take a guess, do you think newts eat tadpoles? Do you know what newts are? [Pause for responses.] If you are curious and want answers to these questions, you'll just have to check out the book *Lily Pad Pond* by Bianca Lavies. By the way, what is a lily pad? (LP-MP)

Have you ever dreamed of flying? The little boy in the story often daydreamed he could fly with the eagles, but one day he found an eagle that could not fly. The eagle had injured his wing. Robin asked his father if they could keep the eagle until its wing mended. Only after the veterinarian looked at the injured bird, and the boy promised to do all his work, did Robin's father say he could help the bird. The eagle remained quite wild as the healing process began.

The boy, Robin, and his mother fed the eagle salmon and watched as it eagerly ate every single fish. The eagle grew stronger. One day Robin was surprised to hear the call of another eagle and to have a salmon fall from that eagle's talons. It was the mate of the injured bird and had remained in the area nearby. What do you think happened when the injured eagle's wing healed? Is Robin able to keep it as a pet? Should he keep it as a pet? Read *Eagle Dreams* by Sheryl McFarlane for a brush with the wild. (UP)

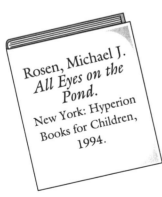

Have you ever fished in a pond? Or had a picnic next to a pond? Ponds are part of our wetlands, and many little creatures live on, in, and around ponds. If you are really quiet and still when you visit a pond, perhaps you will see some of the critters. If you don't see any, you can be sure some of the animals are watching you. Maybe all the eyes of the pond are on you.

This book tells about birds, fish, turtles, bats, and insects that live around the pond, and it gives their particular point of view. Did you know that dragonflies have eyes that make things look like kaleidoscopes and that spiders spy with eight eyes? To learn more about eyes and wildlife around a pond, read *All Eyes on the Pond* by Michael J. Rosen. And on your next visit to a pond, be sure to keep your eyes open. Maybe you'll see something looking back at you. (LP-UP)

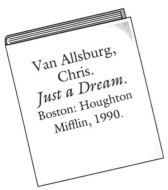

Van Allsburg, Chris. *Just a Dream*. Boston: Houghton Mifflin, 1990.

What do you imagine the future will be like when you are an adult? [Pause to let the children respond.] The little boy in this story thinks it will have robots and little planes. Do any of you think that will happen? Let me tell you what happened to the boy in the story as he dreamed about the future.

First, in real life, this boy did not care about the earth. He tossed his bakery bag on the ground; he did not sort the trash in order to recycle it; and he made fun of the little girl next door when she received a tree as a birthday present. He wasn't a bad little boy. He just had some bad habits.

He had a dream, though, that changed the way he did things. He went to bed one night and dreamed of the future. He expected to see those tiny robots and a little plane and a machine that made jelly doughnuts by the thousands. But what he saw instead scared him. It frightened him so badly he wanted to quit that dream and wake up. Have you ever had a dream like that? [Pause for responses.] If you want to know more about that dream and how this story turns out, you'll have to check out *Just a Dream* by Chris Van Allsburg. Our future may depend on it. (LP-UP)

Bibliography

Asch, Frank. *The Earth and I*. New York: Gulliver Books, 1994.

This book describes how a young child and the earth are friends. The child and the earth sing together, grow together, and listen to one another. A simple story that shows a young child how the earth should be respected. (LP)

Bender, Robert. *A Most Unusual Lunch*. New York: Dial Books for Young Readers, 1994.

A frog swallows a beetle, only to sprout an antennae and six little legs after his lunch. The frog is then swallowed by a fish, who develops some froglike characteristics, plus maintaining the six legs and antennae of the beetle. And so on and so forth throughout the food chain, until the lion gives a tremendous belch, thus reversing the chain. Each individual animal is released from the preceding one in this humorous and elementary account of the food chain. (LP-MP)

Chandrasekhar, Aruna. *Oliver and the Oil Spill*. Kansas City, Mo.: Landmark Editions, 1991.

This 12-year-old author writes about an oil spill and its effects on the marine life. Oliver, an otter pup, is learning what otters do to survive in the ocean. His mother is a good teacher, but one day the water turns black and smells bad. The birds and fish start to die, and the otters become ill. Oliver and his mother are taken to a rescue station, but it is too late to save his mother. This is a well-told story of what occurs during an oil spill. (MP-UP)

Cherry, Lynne. *The Armadillo from Amarillo*. New York: Gulliver Books, 1994.

An armadillo in Texas sets out to find out where in the world he is. He travels from Amarillo to San Antonio to the bluebonnet-covered hills of the countryside. The armadillo corresponds with his cousin via postcards and thus tracks his travels. Finally, he meets up with an eagle. They travel far above Texas, the United States, and the North American continent and finally go into outer space with the space shuttle. Then the armadillo understands where he is from and where he is. (UP)

Cherry, Lynne. *The Great Kapok Tree: A Tale of the Amazon Rain Forest*. San Diego: Harcourt Brace Jovanovich, 1990.

One day, a man enters the rain forest to cut down a kapok tree. As he swings his ax, he becomes tired and takes a nap under the tree.

Each animal that depends on the tree for life whispers into the man's ear as he sleeps. When he awakens, he sees the creatures and plants of the rain forest with new understanding. (LP-UP)

Greene, Carol. *The Old Ladies Who Liked Cats.* New York: HarperCollins, 1991.

This environmental tale describes the consequences of disturbing the ecology of an island. The trouble starts when the mayor declares that cats may not be let out at night. This allows the mice to roam freely. The mice eat the honeycomb, which has startling results. The old ladies do end up as the heroes, however. (LP-UP)

Guiberson, Brenda Z. *Cactus Hotel.* New York: Henry Holt, 1991.

The story of a saguaro, the giant of the Sonoran Desert, is told from seed to decay. The story includes all the life forms that prosper from the saguaro's long and productive life. This is a good book to use to introduce children to the ecology of the Sonoran Desert. (UP)

Hall, Derek. *Otter Swims.* New York: Alfred A. Knopf, 1984.

A young otter learns from its mother in this simply told and illustrated story. Otter learns to swim, catch fish, and dry off in the grass. The illustrations add to the charm of this book. (LP-MP)

Hamilton, Virginia. *Jaguarundi.* New York: Blue Sky Press, 1995.

When the settlers come and the rain forest disappears, it is time for Rundi Jaguarundi and Coati Coatimundi to decide what to do. They meet with all the other animals of the region and listen to the advice of the big brown bat to adapt. Jaguarundi and Coati decide to travel north and seek the shelter of the Rio Bravo. They meet other creatures on the way, but in the end find that they too must adapt, and hope for a better future. Thumbnail sketches are provided of many of the rain forest animals. (UP)

Jordon, Martin. *Journey of the Red-Eyed Tree Frog.* New York: Green Tiger Press, 1992.

Two red-eyed tree frogs, Hops-a-Little and Jumps-a-Little, hear from two toucans that their island home is threatened by development. Hops-a-Little sets out to visit the great wise toad in the depths of the Amazon forest. Along the way Hops-a-Little meets many of the animals threatened by people and learns that in order to survive, we all must share this earth. (UP)

Jordon, Martin. *Jungle Days, Jungle Nights.* New York: Kingfisher Books, 1993.

This book describes the dry season and the wet season in the rain forest of South America. The illustrations are lush, and much information is given about the wildlife found in the rain forest. (UP)

Lauber, Patricia. *You're Aboard Spaceship Earth.* New York: HarperCollins, 1996.

An easy-to-read science book that explains why we can look at our earth as a spaceship. The book explains that the principal needs of food, water, and oxygen, required on a spaceship, are provided for us on earth. It provides an easy-to-understand explanation of the water cycle, and makes the point that the earth will continue to provide for our needs as long as we take care of it. (LP-UP)

Lavies, Bianca. *Lily Pad Pond.* New York: E. P. Dutton, 1989.

The photographs of the life forms in and around the pond are informative and sometimes amusing. The text provides information in an easy-to-read format. (LP-MP)

McFarlane, Sheryl. *Eagle Dreams.* New York: Philomel, 1994.

A boy, Robin, lives on a farm. One day, he discovers an eagle with a broken wing. His father wishes to put the eagle out of its misery, but Robin prevails and nurses the eagle back to health with salmon and loving attention. The illustrations contribute positively to the story and provide a sense of wildness. (UP)

Newton-John, Olivia. *A Pig Tale*. New York: Simon & Schuster Books for Young Readers, 1993.

A story told in rhyme of Ziggy's father, a pig named Iggy, who saved everything and never threw anything away. One day he combined all his "junk" into a magical wonderful invention. The moral of this story is that you too might find something wonderful by conserving, and you could help the earth as well. (LP-MP)

Pallotta, Jerry. *The Desert Alphabet Book*. Watertown, Mass.: Charlesbridge Publishing, 1994.

Each letter represents an animal or plant or feature of the desert. The description of these desert creatures also tells how they are adapted to survive the harshness of the desert. The illustrations are very attractive and colorful. (MP-UP)

Peet, Bill. *Farewell to Shady Glade*. Boston: Houghton Mifflin, 1966.

Although the population of Shady Glade was no more than 16, when the bulldozers came rumbling in the few rabbits, possum, skunk, frogs, and an old raccoon had to relocate. This book is the story of their adventure in finding a new home. (MP-UP)

Radcliffe, Theresa. *The Snow Leopard*. New York: Viking, 1994.

This book describes the fight for survival of a mother snow leopard, Samu, and her cub, Ka. Mountain sheep provide their food until the wolves come to the mountain valley. Samu and Ka must move on to find new sources of food. Their journey is depicted beautifully due to the skill of the illustrator, John Butler. (UP)

Rosen, Michael J. *All Eyes on the Pond*. New York: Hyperion Books for Children, 1994.

Water striders, snails, turtles, crawdads, and all other creatures that live around the pond view their surroundings through their own eyes. This book examines each animal's unique way of viewing and contributing to the life at the pond. (LP-UP)

Ryder, Joanne. *Earth Dance*. New York: Henry Holt, 1996.

Through lyrical verse and colorful illustrations, this book celebrates the planet earth. It celebrates its cities, its people, its day, and its night. It is a joyful tribute to our planet. (LP-MP)

Stone, Lynn. *Amazing Rain Forest: Rain Forests*. Vero Beach, Fla.: Rourke Corporation, 1994.

A combination of photographs and text provide an abundance of information about the rain forest in an easy-to-understand manner. Possible new vocabulary words are printed in bold, and a glossary is provided. (UP)

Van Allsburg, Chris. *Just a Dream*. Boston: Houghton Mifflin, 1990.

As the title indicates, this book is about a dream. It is a vision of the future that a very careless little boy dreams. It turns out to be an environmental nightmare, pictured in a way that only Chris Van Allsburg can illustrate. This dreamy view of the future raises the conscience of the little boy, and he becomes environmentally responsible. (LP-UP)

Van Laan, Nancy. *Round and Round Again*. New York: Hyperion Books for Children, 1994.

This delightful book captures the creativity of recycling in a enchanting way. Written in lively rhyme, the story tells how Mama takes old papers and creates puppets and hats, or how she makes a new house using barn sides and worn-out doors. (LP-UP)

Wheeling Across the Curriculum

Art

- Ask the children to make a "We Love the Earth" poster. (LP-UP)

- Give each child a toilet paper tube, and have them recycle the tube into something else. (LP-UP)

- Make a collage from "found materials." (LP-UP)

- Since art projects have lots of leftover materials, ask the children to come up with suggestions about how to recycle old art materials. (UP)

Language Arts

- Have the children write a letter to the local paper about environmental concerns. (UP)

- Ask the students to name their favorite wild animal. Have them look for that animal in an endangered species reference source. (UP)

- Have the younger children dictate five things they can do to take care of the earth. (LP)

- Have a group of children write a poem about an endangered animal. (MP-UP)

- Ask the children to come up with five questions they want answered about the earth. Ask older children to find the answers to the questions and compile a group book entitled, *Everything We Wanted to Know About the Earth.* (LP-UP)

- Provide the setting and plot for a puppet show. Setting: A pond. Plot: A careless man dumps his leftover paint into the pond. Children will improvise a play with the characters of Frog, Turtle, and Dragonfly. You can make up any characters and let the children act it out. (MP-UP)

Mathematics

- Collect information about the highest mountains on earth. Use graph paper to demonstrate how a 14,000-foot mountain would look as compared to a 24,000-foot mountain.

- Then collect information about the lowest places on earth. Graph two or three of these locations. Have the children calculate the difference between the highest point on earth and the lowest point. (UP)

Music

- Provide tapes of nature sounds, such as whales spouting or wolves howling. Ask the children what other earth sounds they can think of—perhaps wind or rain? (LP-UP)

Reading

- Post articles from the newspaper that tell about ecological issues. (UP)

- Have the children read about an area that is ecologically different from their own. (MP-UP)

- Have the children make a mural depicting the environment they chose to read about. (UP)

- Have the children enter earth words in a group dictionary, words such as pollution, ecology, or biome. (MP-UP)

Science

- Get a copy of your community' recycling program. What are the categories ? Glass? Paper? Plastic? Have the children make a poster illustrating what items are recyclable. (MP-UP)

- Pass around a cactus and a broad-leafed house plant. Have the children guess where each plant might grow. Have the children compare the two. For example: Which plant can they touch? Which plant can store water? Which plant would dry up faster in the hot sun? (MP-UP)

- Ask the students to bring something from the earth that they treasure, such as a rock, seashell, pine cone, or bird feather.

- Display the collection of earth's treasures. Have the students examine the collection with magnifying glasses. (LP-UP)

Social Studies

- Have children as a group make a book entitled *Where I Live*. If you have the computer capabilities, share the pages over the Internet. (LP)

- Discuss responsibility. Who is responsible for taking care of the earth? Use Chris Van Allsburg's *Just a Dream* as a discussion starter. (MP-UP)

Explore Asia

Reference Skills (MP-UP)

Directions: Choose a country in Asia that you would like to know more about. Use a children's atlas and fill in the blanks.

Name of the Country _____

Population _____

Fact 1: _____

Fact 2: _____

Fact 3: _____

Fact 4: _____

Fact 5: _____

Helping Hands

Art (LP-UP)

Directions: Trace around your hand and color it. Print your name above your hand, then finish the promise statement by writing what you will do for the planet earth.

I promise to take care of my planet by

_____

_____

_____

Picture This!

Reading (LP)

Directions: Draw a picture of something that goes with the letter before the frame. The object you draw should be one of your favorite things about the earth.

E

A

R

T

H

.⬛⬛ SUMMER, FALL, WINTER, SPRING: THE SEASONS

CHAPTER 15

Across the country, throughout the year, we repeat the wonderful cycle of seasons. Each region of the country experiences the seasons in its own unique way. Whether it is the mud season indicating the arrival of spring in Vermont, or the monsoon rains rumbling across the desert of Arizona, each area has its own customs and activities to go with their celebration of the seasons.

The books included in this chapter celebrate the seasons in a variety of ways. From fairy tale to photo essay, the books will open the children's eyes to the changes around them.

A Rolling Start

1. To begin the study of the seasons, have the children view a videotape that portrays the four seasons. After viewing the video, ask the children to think about what signs indicate a change of seasons in their own area. Record their responses and categorize them under the headings "Summer," "Fall," "Winter," and "Spring."

2. To increase the children's observations of seasonal changes, ask them the following questions: Does it rain in all seasons? Does it snow in all seasons? (It does if you live at a high altitude or far northern latitude.) Can you grow a garden in the winter? (You can in Phoenix.) Which season is the windiest?

3. These questions will stimulate the children's thinking and curiosity. The books listed in this chapter will help to increase the children's awareness and appreciation of the changing seasons.

Booktalks

Andersen, Hans Christian. *The Snow Queen.* Retold by Richard Hess. New York: Macmillan, 1985.

Have you ever had a piece of dirt or dust fly in your eye? It blurs your vision, doesn't it? Kai, the boy in the fairy tale of the snow queen, has something in his eye, but it does much more than change his vision. It changes his life. What flies into his eye is a bit of mirror that turns everything good into something bad, and vice versa. Kai's good friend, Gerda, doesn't understand why Kai goes from being sweet and loving to being mischievous. When he is taken away to the Ice Palace by the Snow Queen, Gerda pursues Kai. While searching for Kai, Gerda

143

encounters a good witch who wants Gerda to stay with her. The good witch puts a spell on her. When the spell is broken, Gerda is led by crows to the palace of the princess. From there she travels to the robbers' cave. Here her life is spared because of a robber girl who wishes to have a friend. After hearing Gerda's story of her search for Kai, the robber girl sets Gerda free and sends her with a reindeer to search for Kai in Lapland. After meeting various other characters, Gerda finally sees Kai in the Ice Palace. He is playing with a puzzle, which, if he solves it, will gain him his freedom. What is the puzzle? Will Gerda help him, or will she be captured by the Snow Queen? Be sure to read *The Snow Queen* by Hans Christian Andersen to find out if the ending is "happily ever after."(UP)*

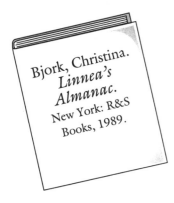

Bjork, Christina. *Linnea's Almanac.* New York: R&S Books, 1989.

Do you know how to make a Swedish heart basket, or create an autumn crown from leaves? Do you know why leaves turn yellow, and how to play gutterball? Instructions, information, and activities fill *Linnea's Almanac*. Who's Linnea, and what is an almanac, you ask? Linnea is a city girl who received *The Old Farmer's Almanac* for Christmas one year. This book tells you everything about weather, crops, and moon cycles throughout the whole year. Linnea decides that she would like to make her own personal almanac, about where she lives in the city. Her two elderly neighbors, Mr. Bloom and Mr. Brush, give Linnea some information to include in her almanac.

If you like birds, weather, arts, crafts, kites, or recipes, you'll be sure to check out *Linnea's Almanac* by Christina Bjork, and join her month by month throughout her year. Who knows? Maybe you'll even end up writing YOUR OWN almanac. (MP-UP)*

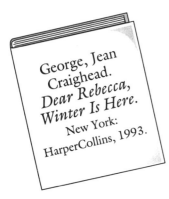

George, Jean Craighead. *Dear Rebecca, Winter Is Here.* New York: HarperCollins, 1993.

What clues do you use to tell that winter has arrived? Do you look for snow, or icicles, or Christmas trees?

Rebecca's grandmother writes to Rebecca to tell her all the signs that she has observed to indicate that winter is here. The letter Grandma writes is dated December 21st. Do you know what makes December 21st important? [Pause for the children to respond.] It is the winter solstice. Rebecca's grandmother explains to Rebecca that June 21st, the summer solstice, was the longest day of the year. Right after the summer solstice, days become shorter, until we arrive at December 21st, the shortest day, and the beginning of winter. The letter goes on to tell Rebecca how winter will affect the birds, the animals, and even Rebecca. Rebecca will wear mittens, and play in the snow, and even make snow angels. How many of you have ever made a snow angel?

If you like winter, and if you like really fine illustrations of animals and birds in winter, you should definitely read *Dear Rebecca, Winter Is Here,* by Jean Craighead George. (MP-UP)

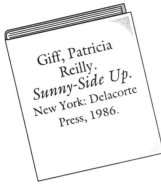

Giff, Patricia Reilly. *Sunny-Side Up.* New York: Delacorte Press, 1986.

Who would title a book *Sunny-Side Up?* Do you think it is a book about eggs? In a way you'd be right, because the characters in the book do try to fry an egg on the sidewalk, sunny-side up. But this book is about a group of kids having a great summer vacation. That is, until Beast, one of the kids, re-members he has to go to summer school. That's not too bad, though, because the other kids, Matthew, Holly, and Emily are also at school. Then Matthew finds out that his family is moving. Not down the street or even in town, but far away. That's when Beast decides Matthew will live in his garage.

Do the kids from Polk Street School get away with this scheme? You'll just have to read this fun-filled chapter book, *Sunny-Side Up* by Patricia Reilly Giff, to find out. (MP-UP)*

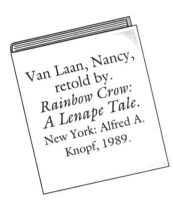

Van Laan, Nancy, retold by. *Rainbow Crow: A Lenape Tale.* New York: Alfred A. Knopf, 1989.

The earth had always been warm for the animals in the forest, but one day the weather changed. Can you guess what hap-pened? On that day snow started falling, and falling, and falling, until the animals stood on each other's backs to keep their heads above the snow. The rabbits sat on the deer's back, and the mice sat on the rabbit's back. The animals knew someone would have to leave earth and go to the Great Sky Spirit to ask him to stop the snow. Who should go? Many animals were suggested—owl, raccoon, coyote—the animals argued and howled and could not agree. And all the while it continued to snow. The snow just grew deeper and deeper.

At last a sweet voice said, "I will go and ask the Sky Spirit to stop the snow." It was Rainbow Crow, offering to go. Rainbow Crow had beauti-ful, colorful feathers, not like the black crows of today.

The animals, anxious to have the snow stop, were happy to see Rainbow Crow fly high into the sky. Rainbow Crow flew high above the earth, the sky, and even the stars.

Finally he reaches the Great Sky Spirit. What happened to Rainbow Crow and the other animals? Why are crows that you see today black and not rainbow-colored? You'll find the surprising explanation when you read *Rainbow Crow: A Le-nape Tale* by Nancy Van Laan. (LP-UP)

Bibliography

Anderson, Hans Christian. *The Snow Queen.* Retold by Richard Hess. New York: Macmillan, 1985.

The season of winter is a major compo-nent of this fairy tale, *The Snow Queen.* Ger-da's attempt to find and save Kai from the Ice Palace leads her to a good witch, a band of robbers, and a Finnish lady. Mix in some crows and a reindeer and you're off on a won-derful adventure. (UP)*

Aylesworth, Jim. *One Crow: A Counting Rhyme.* New York: J. B. Lippincott, 1988.

This book counts to 10, starting with one crow, and ending with 10 children playing. Farm inhabitants are the counting objects. It repeats this count to 10 in two seasons, sum-mer and winter. (LP)

Bjork, Christina, *Linnea's Almanac*. New York: R&S Books, 1989.

Linnea, a young girl, receives *The Old Farmer's Almanac* as a gift from her neighbor, an older gentleman. This inspires her to write her own almanac as she observes the year in its seasons. This book has information on everything, just as a *Farmer's Almanac* should, but it is written in language simple enough for children. (MP-UP)*

Branley, Franklyn. *Sunshine Makes the Seasons*. New York: Thomas Y. Crowell, 1985.

Why do we have seasons? If you want to know the answer to that question, this book will tell you in a clear, understandable manner. Using an orange, a pencil, and a flashlight, you can create an easily understood model of the relationship between the sun's position and the earth. (MP-UP)

Brutschy, Jennifer. *Winter Fox*. New York: Alfred A. Knopf, 1993.

This is a winter story of a gift of a rabbit, a girl's loving care of that rabbit, and a hungry fox in winter. When Anabelle the rabbit is missing, the little girl learns a very hard lesson. (MP-UP)

Busch, Phyllis. *Backyard Safaris: 52 Year Round Science Adventures*. New York: Simon & Schuster Books for Young Readers, 1995.

This book contains science activities that are organized by season. Winter activities range from observing constellations in the winter sky to watching birds feeding at a feeder. Children will surely enjoy reading about and trying these activities for all seasons. (MP-UP)

Chapman, Cheryl. *Snow, on Snow, on Snow*. New York: Dial Books for Young Readers, 1994.

A snowy day adventure takes an African American boy, his dog, and friends outside into the snow. Everyone has fun sledding until the dog is lost, only to be found happily "ever after, ever after, ever after." Repetitive phrases are used throughout the book. (LP)

Cushman, Doug. *Mouse and Mole and the Year Round Garden*. New York: W. H. Freeman, 1994.

As mole plants a garden, mouse learns how things grow. They both watch it through the seasons. Each page has a box at the bottom, with scientific information about subjects such as "winter at the pond," "firefly light," and "how seeds are planted." (MP-UP)

Fowler, Susi Gregg. *When Summer Ends*. New York: Greenwillow Books, 1989.

If everything good happens in the summer, wouldn't *you* cry when it comes to an end? The little girl in this story feels very sad that summer is ending, but with subtle hints from her mother she also remembers the good parts of all the seasons. (LP-MP)

George, Jean Craighead. *Dear Rebecca, Winter Is Here*. New York: HarperCollins, 1993.

A wonderful explanation of the solstice is presented. A grandmother writes to her granddaughter explaining that winter has arrived. Grandmother takes care to reveal just what that event means to Rebecca, the bees, the bears, and the snow birds. (MP-UP)

Giff, Patricia Reilly. *Sunny-Side Up*. New York: Delacorte Press, 1986.

A summer to discover all about swimming, summer school, and losing a best friend to a move. Emily, Holly, Beast, and Matthew are four kids who really take time to enjoy their summer vacation. (MP-UP)*

Kroll, Steven. *I Love Spring*. New York: Holiday House, 1987.

Mark loves spring, and this book lists the reasons why. It covers the natural signs of spring as well as the holidays, including Easter, Passover, Memorial Day, and even Mark's birthday. (LP).

Lucas, Barbara. *Snowed In*. New York: Bradbury Press, 1993.

A picture book that tells the story of a pioneer family in Wyoming. It shows what activities the children pursue from fall to spring when they are *Snowed In*. (LP)

Maas, Robert. *When Autumn Comes.* New York: Henry Holt., 1990.

When autumn arrives, all kinds of things begin to happen: birds fly south; school begins; wood is cut; and the chimney is cleaned. Each autumn activity is described and fully illustrated with a photograph of this season. (LP-UP)

McCauley, Jane R. *Animals in Summer.* Washington, D.C.: National Geographic Society, 1988.

This book is part of the series Books for Young Explorers. It gives an overview of the activities of various animals, insects, birds, and reptiles in the summer. There are photographs, facts, and suggested activities. (MP-UP)

Muller, Gerda. *Around the Oak.* New York: Dutton Children's Books, 1994.

The children pay a visit to Nick, who lives in the middle of a forest because his father is a forest ranger. During several visits, the children learn about the forest in a variety of seasons. (LP-UP)

Owen, Roy. *The Ibis and the Egret.* New York: Philomel, 1993.

The Ibis and Egret sit at the edge of the pond and discuss their favorite season. They come to the conclusion that each season is special and they are all their favorites. Egret, the wise bird, declares that appreciating what one has is the secret of contentment. (LP-UP)

Provensen, Alice and Martin Provensen. *The Year at Maple Hill Farm.* New York: Atheneum, 1978.

This book follows the animals of the farm throughout the year. The reader senses the seasons and the events associated with each season. (LP-UP)

Rockwell, Anne. *Ducklings and Polliwogs.* New York: Macmillan, 1994.

The story starts at the frozen pond in the winter, when a little girl and her father go ice skating. They return to the pond in the spring, and again in the summer and fall. They note the seasonal changes in the creatures that live around the pond. (MP)

Rockwell, Anne. *Apples and Pumpkins.* New York: Macmillan, 1989.

A simple story of autumn, a little girl's visit to the farm, and Halloween. You can guess where the apples and pumpkins come into the story. (LP)

Simon, Seymour. *Autumn Across America.* New York: Hyperion Books for Children, 1993.

This nonfiction book follows autumn across our land from the autumnal equinox to the winter solstice. It is jam-packed with facts and beautiful photographs. There is a companion book titled *Winter Across America* by Seymour Simon. (UP)

Singer, Marilyn. *Turtle in July.* New York: Macmillan, 1989.

Creatures tell of the seasons through their poems. The dog sings of April, the bullhead fish tells its story through all the seasons, and the cow moos out to June. Which month does the cat prefer? (LP-UP)

Turner, Anne. *A Moon for All Seasons.* New York: Macmillan, 1994.

Following the moon through each season, this book contains short poems for each season and beautiful illustrations to enhance the poetic images. (MP-UP)

Van Laan, Nancy, retold by. *Rainbow Crow: A Lenape Tale.* New York: Alfred A. Knopf, 1989.

This Native American tale explains how it was the rainbow crow who saved the other animals of the forest from the unending snows of winter. It also gives the reason why today's crow, though appearing black, has lovely rainbows in its feathers. (LP-UP)

Walt Disney's Bambi. New York: Twin Books, 1989.

It's springtime in the forest and a young rabbit shouts out the news—Bambi has been born. Follow the fawn through the seasons as he experiences winter, spring, summer, and fall, as well as triumph and tragedy. (MP-UP)

Wells, Rosemary. *Night Sounds, Morning Colors.* New York: Dial Books for Young Readers. 1994.

This quiet book tell the story of a little boy and the seasons of his life. Whether he is waking up and describing what he sees or going out with his brother on a cold wintry day, the prose is gentle and fits the illustrations beautifully. (MP)

Yerxa, Leo. *Last Leaf First Snowflake to Fall.* New York: Orchard, 1994.

A Native American parent and child travel through the forests, rivers, and ponds of an untouched natural world, until the moment when the last leaf falls and winter arrives, creating a new world. The collage illustrations greatly add to this book. (LP-UP)

Wheeling Across the Curriculum

Art

- Assign each child a season. Have the child select three crayon colors that he or she thinks represents that season and draw a picture to go with that season. (MP-UP)

- Collect dried weeds in the appropriate season. Direct the children to glue them to construction paper to form a bouquet and then glue a semicircle cut from wallpaper onto the paper as the vase. (LP-UP)

- For a spring activity, have the children use butcher paper to make a giant flower. They can follow these steps.

  1. Draw a 8–10″ circle for the center of the flower. Draw it larger if need be.

  2. Have the children dip their hands into pie tins that contain pink or yellow tempera.

  3. Instruct the children to place their "petal" handprints around the circle, alternating pink and yellow.

  4. Appoint children to paint a stem and leaves for their giant flower.

  5. Print "Celebrate Spring" on your giant posie and hang it in a place of honor. (LP)

Language Arts

- Have the children act out *Rainbow Crow* by Nancy Van Laan. (MP-UP)

- Have the children brainstorm a list of seasonal weather words. Use it for spelling practice. (MP)

- Have the children make up an ABC list using a seasonal word for each letter. The children can illustrate each word and combine the letters for an ABC book. (LP)

- Let the children imagine what people did before there was central heating or air conditioning. Have them write stories about imaginings. (UP)

- Record a dictated story about each child's favorite season. (LP-UP)

- Videotape each child reciting a seasonal poem. Have each child make a prop. (UP)

Mathematics

- A theme of seasons lends itself to calendar work. Give each child a calendar. Have each child, or a team, calculate how many days are in each season. How many weeks? How many months? (MP-UP)

- Make a list of the holidays found in each season. Which season has the most holidays? (LP)

- Graph children's birthdays by seasons. In which season were most children born? (LP-MP)

- Collect leaves in the fall. Trace around them and have the children make patterns. (MP)

- Count the petals on common flowers, such as daisies, petunias, or pansies. Have the children make up addition and subtraction word problems about the flowers.

Music

- Using the tune to "Here We Go 'Round the Mulberry Bush," sing about the seasons. For example, children will sing "Winter is my favorite season, favorite season, favorite season" [repeat]. "And here's the reason why." At that point, the leader can point to a child and have that child give a reason. Continue with each child stating a reason why, or change the seasons as you sing. (LP)

Reading

- As you read various stories, have the children guess the season as part of the setting. (LP-UP)

- Have the children listen to various seasonal poems. What word pictures do they like best? Add these descriptions to your seasonal bulletin board. (MP)

Science

- Devote a corner spot of your reading area to the "SEASON PLACE." This area will be a display area for found objects which represent the season, for example, acorns, leaves, dandelions, icicles, pussy willows, ladybugs, and so on. (LP-UP)

- Make a bird feeder for winter feeding. Use either *Linnea's Almanac* by Christina Bjork or *Backyard Safaris* by Phyllis Busch as a reference. (LP-UP)

- Help the children become scientific observers. Make a list of firsts for each season: First snowfall, first butterfly, first hummingbird, first day over 90° or 100°, or first day below freezing. The list is endless. (LP-UP)

My Family Across the Seasons

Social Studies (LP-MP)

Directions: Draw a picture of your family in each season.

Winter

Fall

Spring

Summer

What to Wear in the Winter

Social Studies (LP)

Directions: Put an *X* on the things that you would wear in the winter. Put an *O* on the clothes that you would wear in the summer.

From *Books on Wheels*. © 1998 Janice McArthur and Barbara E. McGuire. Libraries Unlimited. (800) 237-6124.

Don't Miss This Book!

Reading (MP-UP)

Directions: Make a poster to advertise your favorite book on the seasons. Be sure to include the title, author, and something from the book that will make other kids want to read this book.

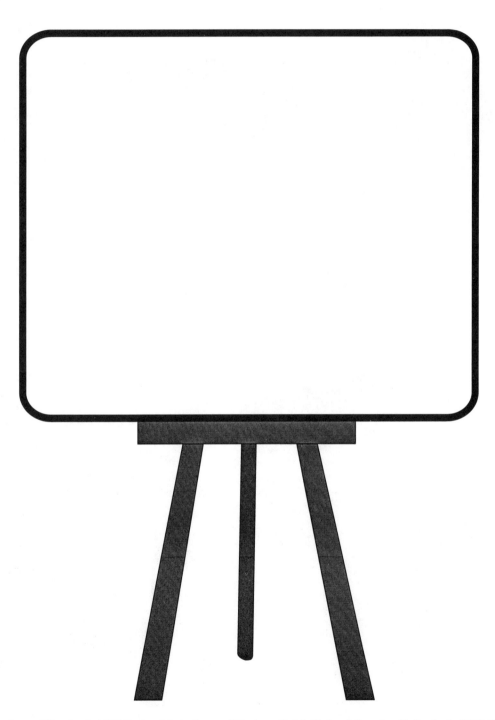

In young children's lives, many changes take place, and events occur that are hard for them to understand. They start school, younger siblings may join the family, and relatives as well as pets may die. In today's mobile society, they may move many times, losing and making new friends several times in a few short years. Events such as these affect a child's feelings of self-worth and self-esteem.

The books in this chapter have been selected to help children strengthen their inner feelings and learn how to accept the events in their lives. The books may also help them realize there are others who have had the same experiences and feelings as they have or are in the same situation.

A Rolling Start

1. Choose one of the Reading Rainbow videos listed below to introduce this theme:

    Gila Monsters Meet You at the Airport by Marjorie Weinman Sharmat
    Arthur's Eyes by Marc Brown
    Keep the Lights Burning, Abbie by Peter Roop and Connie Roop

2. Construct an "All About Us" bulletin board. Children can bring baby photographs of themselves and current pictures. If one is available, an instant camera can be used to take the current picture. Display the pictures with children's names underneath and a sentence that tells something about the child.

3. Create a "My Book." Using a generic shape of a person, cut a cover out of construction paper. Inside, put lined sheets of paper. Ask children to write on different subjects that tell about themselves. Some topics might be: "What I like to do after school," "My hobbies," "What I want to be when I grow up," or "If I had three wishes . . ."

Booktalks

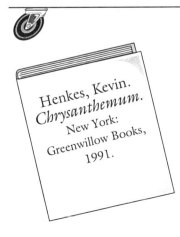

Henkes, Kevin.
Chrysanthemum.
New York:
Greenwillow Books,
1991.

How would you like to be named after a flower? Do you think people's names are important? Are you named after anyone?

When Chrysanthemum was born, her parents thought they had found the perfect name for their little girl. Chrysanthemum loved her name as she grew bigger. Then she started school. The other girls in the class made fun of her name, saying, "It's too long; it has thirteen letters; she isn't named after anyone; and she has the name of a flower." These remarks made Chrysanthemum feel so bad that she didn't want to go to school. Each night when she went home, her mom and dad told her that her name was perfect, that it fit her, then they hugged and kissed her. This made her feel happy again and proud of her name. But when she went to school the next day, the teasing started all over again. Chrysanthemum began to wish she could change her name.

One day Chrysanthemum's class met Mrs. Twinkle, the music teacher. She thought Chrysanthemum's name was wonderful. Chrysanthemum found out that she and Mrs. Twinkle shared something special, which made her very happy. To find out what she shared with Mrs. Twinkle, read *Chrysanthemum* by Kevin Henkes. (LP)

Lowell, Susan. *The Three Little Javelinas.* Flagstaff, Ariz.: Northland. 1992.

Did you know there are wild pigs? In the southwestern part of the United States, there are pigs that run wild in the desert. They are called by their Spanish name *javelina* (ha-ve-LEE-na). This is the story of three javelinas, two brothers and a sister who left home to find their way in the world.

When they come to a fork in the road, each goes its separate way. Soon a coyote finds the first brother, who has built a house. Now, everyone who knows coyotes knows that they like to eat javelinas. Everyone also knows that coyotes are sneaky and use magic to get what they want. Coyote decides that he is going to use his magic to get the javelina, so he huffs and he puffs and blows the javelina's house away. What do you think happens? Does this story sound like another story you are familiar with? [Pause for responses.] You are right; this is a southwestern "three little pigs" story. To find out if the coyote is able to use his magic to get the javelina, and to discover what happens to his brother and sister, read *The Three Little Javelinas* by Susan Lowell. (UP)

Martin, Rafe. *The Rough-Face Girl.* New York: G. P. Putnam's Sons, 1992.

Do you feel that your dreams will never come true? That life is hard and you must do the work for the family? That is what happens in this story.

There once was a young maiden of the Algonquin tribe. She had a father and two older sisters. She spent most of her time cooking for them around the fire. Because of this, her hair and face were burned and charred. Her sisters meanly called her Rough Face.

Rough Face dreamed of marrying the Invisible Being, who was looking for a bride. Her sisters demanded that their father obtain what was needed for them to make new clothes of buckskin and other fine things. They were selfish and took everything for themselves.

Rough Face asked her father if she could have new clothes to look for the Invisible Being. But he told her there was nothing left. So she made herself clothes from things of the earth and started on her quest to find the Invisible Being. Will Rough Face be successful? What will happen if she finds him? Read *The Rough Face Girl* by Rafe Martin to find out. (UP)

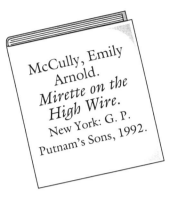

How many of you have been to a circus and seen the people who walk on the thin wire high up in the air?

This is a story that took place in Paris over one hundred years ago. Paris was full of circus and street performers from all over the world. Mirette lived with her mother, who ran a boarding house where many of these people rented rooms. One day, when Mirette went to the courtyard to get the laundry, she saw a man walking across the courtyard on air. What was he doing? It was Senor Bellini, a retired high wire artist. As she watched, Mirette knew she had to learn too. She practiced until she could walk on the wire without falling. Then she showed Bellini what she could do. Bellini agreed to teach her. Then he said he could never do the tricks he used to do because he was afraid.

One day Bellini decides he must try again to walk the wire. Will he be successful? Can he show Mirette that he isn't afraid? What will Mirette do? Will she be able to walk on the wire when it is high in the air? Would you want to walk on the wire? When you read *Mirette on the High Wire* by Emily Arnold McCully you will find out what happens to Mirette and Senor Bellini. (MP-UP)

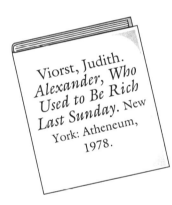

Have you ever had a time when you did not have any money? You just couldn't hang on to it? Instead, you spend it almost as soon as you get it? That is how Alexander feels.

Alexander thinks life is unfair because his brothers have money and he doesn't. All he has are bus tokens! This makes him feel bad.

Then Grandma Betty and Grandpa Louie come to visit on Sunday. Upon their arrival, they give Alexander and his two brothers a dollar each. This makes Alexander feel rich, but the feeling doesn't last long. During the week, many adventures happen to Alexander, and his money dwindles fast, and by the end of the week, he is no longer rich. What happens to Alexander? Where does his money go? In order to find out, read *Alexander, Who Used to Be Rich Last Sunday* by Judith Viorst. (UP)

Bibliography

Aliki. *Best Friends Together Again*. New York: Greenwillow Books, 1995.

Peter and Robert were best friends, but Robert moved away. Robert is excited because Peter is coming for a two-week visit. The boys have a wonderful time and reunite with all their old friends. However, two weeks pass all too quickly for the two best friends. (LP-MP)

Aliki. *Feelings*. New York: Greenwillow Books, 1984.

Everyone has feelings. We feel excited, happy, shy, and many other feelings. This book helps children explore their feelings and learn about friendship. (LP)

Bourgeois, Paulette. *Franklin in the Dark*. New York: Scholastic, 1995.

What is Franklin to do? He is scared of dark, tiny places. Even his own shell is a scary place. How will Franklin solve this problem? (LP)

Bourgeois, Paulette. *Franklin Is Bossy*. New York: Scholastic, 1993.

Franklin likes to play games with his friends. But what happens when he gets too bossy? Do his friends still want to play with him? (LP)

Bourgeois, Paulette. *Franklin Is Messy*. New York: Scholastic, 1994.

Franklin's room is always a mess. He never puts anything away, and therefore he can't ever find anything, either. What helps Franklin decide that being neat is better? (LP)

Bourgeois, Paulette. *Franklin Plays the Game*. New York: Scholastic, 1995.

Franklin loves to play soccer. His only problem is that he has trouble kicking the ball straight. However, because Franklin wants to be an outstanding soccer player, he keeps practicing. He learns several lessons as he practices to improve his game. (LP)

Cannon, Janell. *Stellaluna*. San Diego: Harcourt Brace Jovanovich, 1993.

Stellaluna is a baby fruit bat. One night she falls out of the tree and lands in a nest with baby birds. Stellaluna grows up with the baby birds and acts like a bird instead of a bat. What happens when Stellaluna tries to hang upside down and sees some other animals like her? Will she find her mother? (LP-UP)

Carle, Eric. *The Grouchy Ladybug*. New York: Thomas Y. Crowell, 1977.

Did the ladybug get up on the wrong side of the bed? The ladybug is looking for someone to fight with. The size or strength of the person the ladybug challenges doesn't matter. What will finally happen to the ladybug? (MP-UP)

Carle, Eric. *The Mixed-Up Chameleon*. New York: HarperCollins, 1991.

The chameleon can change colors to match whatever he stands next to. However, the chameleon is bored. He wants to be like the other animals he sees. After many changes, he decides that maybe it isn't always best to be something different. (LP-MP)

Carlson, Nancy. *I Like Me!* New York: Puffin, 1993.

Are you your own best friend? This book talks about all the things that you can do to be friends with yourself. It also helps you to feel good about yourself. (LP)

Carlstrom, Nancy White. *Wild, Wild Sunflower Child Anna*. New York : Macmillan, 1987.

Anna uses her imagination to play games, to look at the clouds and see shapes, and to play in the trees and in the sunflowers. She loves the things she sees in her world. (LP)

Giff, Patricia Reilly. *Ronald Morgan Goes to Bat*. New York: Viking Kestrel, 1988.

Ronald loves to play baseball, but he is not a very good player. He has lots of enthusiasm and is willing to practice. Will that help Ronald be a better player? (UP)

Giff, Patricia Reilly. *Watch Out, Ronald Morgan!* New York: Viking Kestrel, 1985.

Ronald makes many mistakes and does funny things because he can't see well. The other children laugh at him. Then Ronald gets glasses and can see well enough to do things correctly. What a difference! (UP)

Gramatky, Hardie. *Little Toot*. New York: Putnam, 1967.

Toot is the littlest tugboat in the harbor. Can he do the work that the large boats do? Little Toot discovers that he has his place in the harbor, just as the larger ships do. (LP-MP)

Grimes, Nikki. *Meet Danitra Brown*. New York: Lothrop, Lee & Shepard, 1994.

"You oughta meet Danitra Brown, the most splendiferous girl in town." What makes Danitra so splendiferous? She is not afraid to take a dare and does wonderful things with her friends. (MP-UP)

Henkes, Kevin. *Chrysanthemum*. New York: Greenwillow Books, 1991.

What's in a name? Chrysanthemum loves her absolutely perfect name until she goes to school, where the children tease her about it. Then Chrysanthemum discovers that her name is wonderful and perfect for her. (LP)

Hines, Anna Grossnickle. *Big Help!* New York: Clarion, 1995.

Lucy wants to help Sam with everything. But as little sisters do, every time Lucy helps, she causes a mess. What will Sam do that will let Lucy help and let him finish his drawing? (LP-MP)

Hoffman, Mary. *Amazing Grace.* New York: Dial Books for Young Readers, 1991.

Grace can do anything she wants! She has a big imagination and tries all kinds of adventures. Because of her courage and faith in herself, she is amazing. (MP)

Jahn-Clough, Lisa. *Alicia Has a Bad Day.* New York: Houghton Mifflin, 1994.

This story is about Alicia and the rotten day she is having. Then something happens that changes it to a not-so-bad day. Things do get better. What is it that happens? (LP-MP)

Joosse, Barbara M. *The Morning Chair.* New York: Clarion, 1995.

Bram moves from Holland to a big new city in America. Nothing is familiar, from the tall, tall buildings to their apartment without furniture. Then their furniture arrives from Holland, with the chair that Bram and Mama used to sit in. Now they sit together in the chair and look out the window and learn about their new life in America. (LP-MP)

Keats, Ezra Jack. *Peter's Chair.* New York: Harper & Row, 1967.

When Peter's new baby sister arrives, she gets lots of attention and some of Peter's baby things. Peter feels left out. He decides that his sister will not get his chair. Then he discovers he is too big for it and it doesn't fit him anymore. (LP)

Kraus, Robert. *Leo, the Late Bloomer.* New York: Windmill, 1971.

Leo feels that he can't do anything right. He doesn't do things when the other children do them. As he grows, Leo's father watches to see if he is blooming. In this story, Leo learns that everyone is different and that he will do things in his own time. (LP)

Lee, Virginia. *Mike Mulligan and His Steam Shovel.* New York: Houghton Mifflin, 1939.

Mike Mulligan and his steam shovel can do anything. They work hard and help many people. One day, they dig the basement for the new city building. What happens when they get stuck? (LP-MP)

Lester, Helen. *Tacky the Penguin.* New York: Houghton Mifflin, 1992.

Tacky isn't like other penguins. He doesn't dress the way they do or walk the way they do. The other penguins don't like him, and don't want to have much to do with him. But then danger occurs, and Tacky saves the day. (LP-UP)

Lionni, Leo. *A Color of His Own.* New York: Pantheon, 1975.

Chameleons aren't like other animals who have colors of their own. Chameleons change colors to match their surroundings. This makes one chameleon very unhappy because he wants his own color. As he searches for his own color, he learns a valuable lesson. (LP)

Lionni, Leo. *Swimmy.* New York: Pantheon Book, 1983.

Swimmy is different than the other fish. He feels upset because of this, but he learns that being different is not always a bad thing. (LP)

Lowell, Susan. *The Three Little Javelinas.* Flagstaff, Ariz.: Northland, 1992.

This is the story of three southwestern javelinas (wild pigs). Two brothers have built their homes out of tumbleweed and cactus spines. Soon these two javelinas are running from the coyote. Will their smart sister, who has built her house out of adobe, be able to save her brothers? (UP)

Martin, Rafe. *The Rough-Face Girl.* New York: G. P. Putnam's Sons, 1992.

This Algonquin tale is about a young girl who is treated badly by her two sisters. Her hair and face are charred from cooking in the fire. Her sisters are mean and call her Rough Face. Will she find happiness? Will her dream come true? (UP)

McCully, Emily Arnold. *Mirette on the High Wire*. New York: G. P. Putnam's Sons. 1992.

This story takes place in Paris over a hundred years ago. Mirette wants to learn how to walk the high wire. Bellini is a world-famous high wire walker. Will he regain his courage so he can teach Mirette how to walk the high wire? (MP-UP)

McKissack, Patricia C. *Flossie and the Fox*. New York: Dial Books for Young Readers, 1986.

Flossie is smart, but she doesn't know what a fox looks like. She does know that they are very smart. Can Flossie be smarter than a fox, should she ever meet one? (MP)

Silverstein, Shel. *The Giving Tree*. New York: Harper & Row, 1964.

This story tells about a tree that gives throughout its life, and the many things it does for the person it loves. (MP)

Viorst, Judith. *Alexander, Who Used to Be Rich Last Sunday*. New York: Atheneum, 1978.

Why doesn't Alexander have any money? He has many adventures with his money and spends it all very quickly. Alexander isn't happy about the way things are going in his life. What can he do to change? (UP)

Weber, Bernard. *Ira Sleeps Over*. Boston: Houghton Mifflin, 1972.

Ira has been invited to spend the night with a friend. He can't decide if he should take his teddy bear. Will his friend make fun of him if he takes his bear? Should he leave it at home? What will Ira decide to do? (MP-UP)

Wheeling Across the Curriculum

Art

- After reading *The Mixed-Up Chameleon* by Eric Carle, children can make their own "mixed-up animal." (MP-UP)

- Children can make a design out of the letters in their names. (LP-UP)

- Make a bulletin board out of all the children's names in the class. (LP-UP)

- Using paper plates, children can make puppets with faces showing different kinds of feelings. (LP-UP)

- Make a collage of pictures cut from magazines showing activities that children like to do. (LP-UP)

- Children can make drawings of activities they like to do with friends and family members. (LP-MP)

- As a group, children can make a mural depicting activities they like to do with family and friends. Example: a mural showing children playing games together. (MP-UP)

- Children can make a collage of pictures showing their favorite activities. (LP-UP)

- Life histories can be written in narrative or story form by the children. The stories can then be shared with family and friends. (UP)

- By looking through magazines, children can find pictures of people showing emotion. The pictures can be placed on a chart and labeled with the appropriate feelings. (MP-LP)

Drama

- Have children role-play various feelings and how to handle them after reading *The Grouchy Ladybug* by Eric Carle or *Feelings* by Aliki. (LP-UP)
- Children can role-play scenarios that deal with different feelings and situations that involve friends and peers. (LP-UP)

Language Arts

- Have children brainstorm a list of all the things they can do. The list could include tying shoes, writing their name in cursive, or playing a game. (LP-UP)
- Instruct the children to make an acrostic poem of their name, using adjectives to describe themselves and their personalities. (LP-UP)
- Children can keep a journal about their feelings. Depending on their ages, this could be done for several days or a week. (MP-UP)

Mathematics

- After making a family or personal time line, children can make up math problems using the numbers and dates on the time line. (UP)

Science

- Thumbprints can be used to show the children that they are unique people and have something that is their own. (MP-UP)

  Examine the children's fingerprints with a magnifying glass, so that the similarities and differences can be seen. (MP-UP)

  Thumbprints of children can be made. Write the slogan "I am Thumb Body" above the print. Thumbprints can be put on a bulletin board or in a class book. (MP-UP)

  Children can make fingerprint families showing their family members. The prints can be made to look like family members, with faces, hair, and clothes added by the children. They can be displayed on a bulletin board. (LP-UP)

Social Studies

- A personal time line showing events in their life can be made by children. The time line can be made with drawings or with photographs. (UP)
- Children make a family time line with pictures showing events in the family, vacations that the family has taken, and so on. (MP-UP)
- Using pictures, children can make histories of their lives. All those old family pictures that their mothers have been saving can be used. (MP-UP)
- An audiotape telling about the life histories can be done by the children. They can also tape the time lines previous listed. (UP)
- Mark on a map all the places where the children or their families have come from. (LP-UP)
- Artifacts are representative of culture. Children can bring something that tells about them, their family, or their culture. (LP-UP)

Alexander, Who Used to Be Rich Last Sunday

by Judith Viorst

Mathematics (MP-UP)

Directions: Draw a picture to represent how much money Anthony has.

Alexander says his brother Anthony has 2 dollars, 3 quarters, 1 dime, 7 nickels, and 18 pennies.

Dollars	Quarters	Dimes	Nickels	Pennies

Alexander was given a dollar ($1.00). He wasn't able to keep it very long.

Directions: Do the following math problems to see where Alexander's money went:

First he spent $.15 on bubble gum.

  How much did he have left?

Next Alexander lost $.15 more on bets he made with his brothers.

  How much did he have left?

Alexander rented Eddie's snake for one hour at $.12 an hour.

  How much did he have left?

Make up a math problem to show how Alexander could spend the rest of his money.

$$
\begin{array}{r}
\$1.00 \\
- \\
\hline
= \\
- \\
\hline
= \\
- \\
= \\
\end{array}
$$

Name Poem

Language Arts (LP-UP)

Directions: In the box below write words that tell about you. There is an example for you. A name poem tells about YOU. Use words that describe you and what you like to do and that start with the letters in your name.

Example:

Name: Jane
  joyful, jolly
  nice, noisy
  excited, enjoys
  jumps, naughty
  jovial, energetic
  always smiling
  a girl

Directions: In the space below write a poem using your name. Sometimes you can use phrases. See the example below.

Example:
  Joyful
  Always Smiling
  Nice
  Energetic

  Jolly
  Interesting
  Mostly Plays

YOUR POEM

Family Crest

Social Studies (LP-UP)

Directions: Divide the crest into four sections. In the first section, draw a picture of something that you like to do. In the second section, draw a picture of the members of your family. In the third section, draw a picture of something that you do as a family, such as camping. In the last section, draw another picture about something of yours, such as your pet.

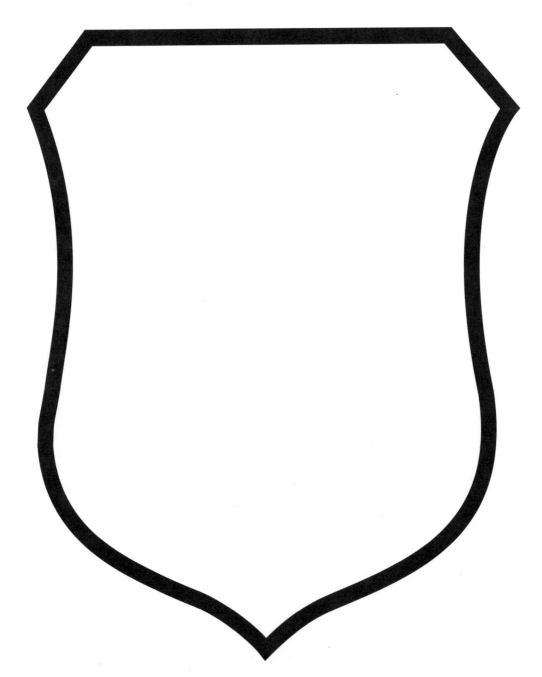

Bold numbers indicate booktalks. Italic numbers indicate curriculum activities.